A NavPress Bible study on the book of

ROMANS

Margo Sprows

732-575-5766

NAVPRESS

A MINISTRY OF THE NAVIGATORS
P.O. BOX 35001, COLORADO SPRINGS, COLORADO 80935

OUR GUARANTEE TO YOU

We believe so strongly in the message of our books that we are making this quality guarantee to you. If for any reason you are disappointed with the content of this book, return the title page to us with your name and address and we will refund to you the list price of the book. To help us serve you better, please briefly describe why you were disappointed. Mail your refund request to: NavPress, P.O. Box 35002, Colorado Springs, CO 80935.

The Navigators is an international Christian organization. Our mission is to reach, disciple, and equip people to know Christ and to make Him known through successive generations. We envision multitudes of diverse people in the United States and every other nation who have a passionate love for Christ, live a lifestyle of sharing Christ's love, and multiply spiritual laborers among those without Christ.

NavPress is the publishing ministry of The Navigators. NavPress publications help believers learn biblical truth and apply what they learn to their lives and ministries. Our mission is to stimulate spiritual formation among our readers.

ISBN 08910-90738

Most Scripture quotations are from the *Holy Bible: New International Version®* (NIV®). Copyright © 1973, 1978, 1984, International Bible Society. Used by permission of Zondervan Bible Publishers. Other versions used are the *New American Standard Bible* (NASB). © The Lockman Foundation 1960, 1962, 1963, 1968, 1971, 1972, 1973, 1975, 1977; the *Revised Standard Version of the Bible* (RSV), copyrighted 1946, 1952, © 1971, 1973; and the *King James Version* (KJV).

Printed in the United States of America

19 20 21 22 23 24 25 / 05 04 03 02 01 00

FOR A FREE CATALOG OF
NAVPRESS BOOKS & BIBLE STUDIES,
CALL 1-800-366-7788 (USA)
or 1-416-499-4615 (CANADA)

CONTENTS

ACKNOWLEDGMENTS

The LIFECHANGE series has been produced through the coordinated efforts of a team of Navigator Bible study developers and NavPress editorial staff, along with a nationwide network of fieldtesters.

SERIES EDITOR: KAREN LEE-THORP

HOW TO USE THIS STUDY

Objectives

Each guide in the LIFECHANGE series of Bible studies covers one book of the Bible. Although the LIFECHANGE guides vary with the individual books they explore, they share some common goals:

1. To provide you with a firm foundation of understanding and a thirst to return to the book;

2. To teach you by example how to study a book of the Bible without structured guides;

3. To give you all the historical background, word definitions, and explanatory notes you need, so that your only other reference is the Bible;

4. To help you grasp the message of the book as a whole;

5. To teach you how to let God's Word transform you into Christ's image.

Each lesson in this study is designed to take 60 to 90 minutes to complete on your own. The guide is based on the assumption that you are completing one lesson per week, but if time is limited you can do half a lesson per week or whatever amount allows you to be thorough.

Flexibility

LIFECHANGE guides are flexible, allowing you to adjust the quantity and depth of your study to meet your individual needs. The guide offers many optional questions in addition to the regular numbered questions. The optional questions, which appear in the margins of the study pages, include the following:

Optional Application. Nearly all application questions are optional; we hope you will do as many as you can without overcommitting yourself.

For Thought and Discussion. Beginning Bible students should be able to handle these, but even advanced students need to think about them. These questions frequently deal with ethical issues and other biblical principles. They often offer cross-references to spark thought, but the references do not give

5

obvious answers. They are good for group discussions.

For Further Study. These include: a) cross-references that shed light on a topic the book discusses, and b) questions that delve deeper into the passage. You can omit them to shorten a lesson without missing a major point of the passage.

(Note: At the end of lessons two through nineteen you are given the option of outlining the passage just studied. Although the outline is optional, you will probably find it worthwhile.)

If you are meeting in a group, decide together which optional questions to prepare for each lesson, and how much of the lesson you will cover at the next meeting. Normally, the group leader should make this decision, but you might let each member choose his or her own application questions.

As you grow in your walk with God, you will find the LIFECHANGE guide growing with you—a helpful reference on a topic, a continuing challenge for application, a source of questions for many levels of growth.

Overview and Details

The guide begins with an overview of the book. The key to interpretation is context—what is the whole passage or book *about?*—and the key to context is purpose—what is the author's *aim* for the whole work? In lesson one you will lay the foundation for your study by asking yourself, Why did the author (and God) write the book? What did they want to accomplish? What is the book about?

Then, in lesson two, you will begin analyzing successive passages in detail. Thinking about how a paragraph fits into the overall goal of the book will help you to see its purpose. Its purpose will help you see its meaning. Frequently reviewing a chart or outline of the book will enable you to make these connections.

Finally, in the last lesson, you will review the whole book, returning to the big picture to see whether your view of it has changed after closer study. Review will also strengthen your grasp of major issues and give you an idea of how you have grown from your study.

Kinds of Questions

Bible study on your own—without a structured guide—follows a progression. First you observe: What does the passage *say?* Then you interpret: What does the passage *mean?* Lastly you apply: How does this truth affect my life?

Some of the "how" and "why" questions will take some creative thinking, even prayer, to answer. Some are opinion questions without clearcut right answers; these will lend themselves to discussions and side studies.

Don't let your study become an exercise of knowledge alone. Treat the passage as God's Word, and stay in dialogue with Him as you study. Pray, "Lord, what do you want me to see here?" "Father, why is this true?" "Lord, how does this apply to my life?"

It is important that you write down your answers. The act of writing clarifies your thinking and helps you to remember.

Meditating on verses is an option in several lessons. Its purpose is to let biblical truth sink into your inner convictions so that you will increasingly be able to act on this truth as a natural way of life. You may want to find a quiet place to spend five minutes each day repeating the verse(s) to yourself. Think about what each word, phrase, and sentence means to you. At intervals throughout the rest of the day, remind yourself of the verse(s).

Study Aids

A list of reference materials, including a few notes of explanation to help you make good use of them, begins on page 209. This guide is designed to include enough background to let you interpret with just your Bible and the guide. Still, if you want more information on a subject or want to study a book on your own, try the references listed.

Scripture Versions

Unless otherwise indicated, the Bible quotations in this guide are from the New International Version of the Bible. Other versions cited are the Revised Standard Version (RSV), the New American Standard Bible (NASB), and the King James Version (KJV).

Use any translation you like for study, preferably more than one. A paraphrase such as The Living Bible is not accurate enough for study, but it can be helpful for comparison or devotional reading.

Memorizing and Meditating

A Psalmist wrote, "I have hidden your word in my heart that I might not sin against you" (Psalm 119:11). If you write down a verse or passage that challenges or encourages you, and reflect on it often for a week or more, you will find it beginning to affect your motives and actions. We forget quickly what we read once; we remember what we ponder.

When you find a significant verse or passage, you might copy it onto a card to keep with you. Set aside five minutes during each day just to think about what the passage might mean in your life. Recite it over to yourself, exploring its meaning. Then, return to your passage as often as you can during your day, for a brief review. You will soon find it coming to mind spontaneously.

For Group Study

A group of four to ten people allows the richest discussions, but you can adapt this guide for other sized groups. It will suit a wide range of group types, such as home Bible studies, growth groups, youth groups, and businessmen's studies.

Both new and experienced Bible students, and new and mature Christians, will benefit from the guide. You can omit or leave for later years any questions you find too easy or too hard.

The guide is intended to lead a group through one lesson per week. However, feel free to split lessons if you want to discuss them more thoroughly. Or, omit some questions in a lesson if preparation or discussion time is limited. You can always return to this guide for personal study later. You will be able to discuss only a few questions at length, so choose some for discussion and others for background. Make time at each discussion for members to ask about anything they didn't understand.

Each lesson in the guide ends with a section called "For the group." These sections give advice on how to focus a discussion, how you might apply the lesson in your group, how you might shorten a lesson, and so on. The group leader should read each "For the group" at least a week ahead so that he or she can tell the group how to prepare for the next lesson.

Each member should prepare for a meeting by writing answers for all the background and discussion questions to be covered. If the group decides not to take an hour per week for private preparation, then expect to take at least two meetings per lesson to work through the questions. Application will be very difficult, however, without private thought and prayer.

Two reasons for studying in a group are accountability and support. When each member commits in front of the rest to seek growth in an area of life, you can pray with one another, listen jointly for God's guidance, help one another to resist temptation, assure each other that the other's growth matters to you, use the group to practice spiritual principles, and so on Pray about one another's commitments and needs at most meetings. Spend the first few minutes of each meeting sharing any results from applications prompted by previous lessons. Then discuss new applications toward the end of the meeting. Follow such sharing with prayer for these and other needs.

If you write down each other's applications and prayer requests, you are more likely to remember to pray for them during the week, ask about them at the next meeting, and notice answered prayers. You might want to get a notebook for prayer requests and discussion notes.

Notes taken during discussion will help you to remember, follow up on ideas, stay on the subject, and clarify a total view of an issue. But don't let note-taking keep you from participating. Some groups choose one member at each meeting to take notes. Then someone copies the notes and distributes them at the next meeting. Rotating these tasks can help include people. Some groups have someone take notes on a large pad of paper or erasable marker board (preformed shower wallboard works well), so that everyone can see what has been recorded.

Page 212 lists some good sources of counsel for leading group studies. *The Small Group Letter,* published by NavPress, is unique, offering insights from experienced leaders every other month.

BACKGROUND

Paul and Rome

Map of the Roman Empire

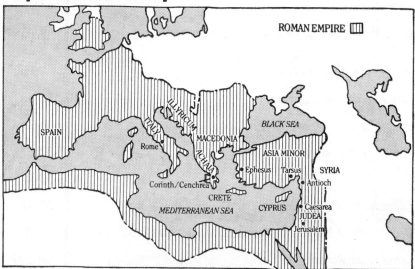

In the prologue to the 1534 edition of his English New Testament, William Tyndale calls the letter to the Romans "the principal and most excellent part of the New Testament" and "an introduction unto all the Old Testament."[1] Why? First, because the letter is the most thorough statement of the gospel that God has given us, and second, because it draws together the whole intent of the Old Testament to explain that gospel.

Tyndale goes on to say, "No man verily can read it too oft or study it too well: for the more it is studied the easier it is, the more it is chewed the pleasanter it is, and the more groundly it is searched the preciouser things are found in it, so great treasure of spiritual things lieth hid therein." How did such a treasure come to be?

Timeline of Paul's Ministry

(All dates are approximate, based on F.F. Bruce, *Paul: Apostle of the Heart Set Free*, page 475.)

Public ministry of Jesus	28-30 AD
Conversion of Paul (Acts 9:1-19)	33
Paul visits Jerusalem to see Peter (Galatians 1:18)	35
Paul in Cilicia and Syria (Galatians 1:21, Acts 9:30)	35-46
Paul visits Jerusalem to clarify the mission to the Gentiles (Galatians 2:1-10)	46
Paul and Barnabas in Cyprus and Galatia (Acts 13-14)	47-48
Letter to the Galatians	48?
Council of Jerusalem (Acts 15)	49
Paul and Silas travel from Antioch to Asia Minor, Macedonia, and Achaia (Acts 16-17)	49-50
Letters to the Thessalonians	50
Paul in Corinth (Acts 18:1-18)	50-52
Paul visits Jerusalem	52
Paul in Ephesus (Acts 19)	52-55
Letters to the Corinthians	55-56
Paul travels to Macedonia, Dalmatia, and Achaia (Acts 20)	55-57
Letter to the Romans	early 57
Paul to Jerusalem (Acts 21:1-23:22)	May 57
Paul imprisoned in Caesarea (Acts 23:23-26:32)	57-59
Paul sent to house arrest in Rome (Acts 27:1-28:31)	59-62
Letters to Philippians, Colossians, Ephesians, Philemon	60?-62
Letters to Timothy and Titus	?
Paul executed in Rome	65?

Looking westward

In 57 AD, Paul had been a missionary apostle for about twenty years. He had spent the past ten years evangelizing Asia Minor, Macedonia, and Greece (Achaia), and he felt his work there was fulfilled. Now that local leaders were equipped to care for the churches Paul had planted, Paul was looking westward to Spain—the farthest end of the Empire, which had never heard the gospel (Romans 15:23-24).

On the way to Spain, Paul hoped to satisfy a longing to visit Rome. Although he was legally a citizen of Rome (Acts 22:27-28), Paul had never seen the famed capital of the Empire. A stay there would be a chance to meet members of the network of churches already flourishing in Rome. Paul hoped that the Roman Christians would help provide funds and a base of operations for his mission to Spain.

However, Paul had met only a few of the hundreds of Christians now living in Rome. Also, he could not journey westward immediately. He had collected a gift of money for the poor Christians in Jerusalem from the Gentile Christians in Greece, and he felt he should deliver it to Jerusalem personally (Romans 15:25-26). For these reasons, he decided to send a letter of introduction to the Roman Christians to prepare them for his visit. The letter Paul wrote from Greece in the early spring of 57 AD (Acts 20:2-3) turned out to be his greatest treatise on the gospel.

Saul the Pharisee

To understand Paul's letter, we should know at least a few of the things the Romans may have heard about the apostle. He was born in the first decade AD in Tarsus, a prosperous city on the trade route from Syria to Asia Minor. Tarsus was known for its schools of philosophy and liberal arts, and Paul may have had some contact with these. Like most cities in the Empire, Tarsus probably contained synagogues of Greek-speaking Jews who were often as devout as their Hebrew-speaking brethren.[2]

However, in Philippians 3:5, Paul calls himself "a Hebrew of Hebrews," which probably means that his parents spoke Hebrew and raised him in a strict Jewish home, isolated as much as possible from the pagan city around them.[3] They named their boy "Saul" after Israel's first king, for the family belonged to King Saul's tribe of Benjamin (Philippians 3:5). They must have owned property and had some importance in the community, for Saul was born not only a citizen of Tarsus (Acts 21:39) but also a citizen of Rome.[4]

Saul was sent to study Jewish Law in Jerusalem under the foremost rabbi of his day, the Pharisee Gamaliel (Acts 22:3, Galatians 1:14). The Pharisees (the Hebrew word means "the separated ones") felt God had set them apart to live by the *Torah* (the Law, or Teaching, of Moses). For them, that meant following the interpretations of the Torah laid down by generations of Jewish teachers. Some Pharisees held that a man was righteous if he had done more good than bad, but Saul apparently followed the more strict group that insisted that every least implication of the Law must be kept.[5]

The Pharisees expected a *Messiah* (Hebrew for "Anointed One"; Greek: *Christ*), who would deliver them from foreign oppression and rule with justice. However, Jesus of Nazareth had infuriated many Pharisees by interpreting the Law differently and acting like God. Thus, when some Jews began to proclaim Jesus as Messiah and Lord (a term usually reserved for God), strict Pharisees opposed them vehemently.

Saul helped to lead the fight against the proclaimers of Christ in Jerusalem (Acts 7:60-8:3, Galatians 1:13). When some were driven out, Saul obtained permission to pursue them to Damascus. But on the way there, Jesus confronted Saul in a blinding encounter (Acts 9:1-19), revealing to Saul that he was persecuting the very God he professed to worship. Saul's life now turned from Pharisaic observance of God's Law to a devoted obedience to Jesus Christ, the revealed Messiah. He joined the Jews who were urging other Jews to believe in Jesus, and shortly thereafter God called him to proclaim Jesus as Savior to Gentiles (non-Jews) also. Saul took the Greek name Paul when he turned to work among Gentiles.

Paul the missionary

Paul's conversion may have marked his first move outward from cloistered Judaism into pagan culture. He spent seven years in Cilicia and Syria (Galatians 1:21), probably preaching Jesus along with Greek-speaking Jewish Christians. Then Barnabas brought Paul from Tarsus to Syrian Antioch, where by this time the church was more Gentile than Jewish.[6]

After some time, the church in Antioch sent Paul and Barnabas to evangelize Cyprus and Galatia for about two years. The missionaries then returned to Antioch, until some teachers came, saying that Gentile Christians must be circumcised and follow the Jewish laws. Paul and Barnabas strongly opposed this teaching, and eventually both they and the Judaizers went to Jerusalem to have the apostles pronounce on the matter. The apostles embraced Paul's view that Gentile Christians had to be moral and avoid idolatry but did not have to keep Jewish customs (Acts 15:1-35). Sadly, this was not the end of the controversy; Paul struggled against Judaizers for years thereafter.

Paul launched another missionary campaign after the Jerusalem council. With Silas and some other companions, Paul spent four years in Asia, Macedonia, and Achaia (Greece). After a quick trip to Jerusalem and Antioch, Paul took a third journey to Ephesus, through Macedonia, and finally to Corinth (Acts 15:40-20:3). In Corinth or the nearby port of Cenchrea, while staying with a man named Gaius (Romans 16:23, 1 Corinthians 1:14), Paul probably wrote to Rome. Shortly thereafter he left Corinth for Jerusalem.

Arrival in Rome

Paul got to Rome, but not in the way he planned. When he appeared in Jerusalem with the alms from his Gentile converts, some Jewish enemies incited the Roman authorities to arrest him. He spent two years in prison in Caesarea, but when a new Roman governor suggested sending Paul to stand trial in a Jewish court, Paul appealed for trial before Caesar (Acts 21:17-25:12).

The trip to Rome took nearly a year because of a storm and shipwreck (Acts 27:1-28:16), so Paul arrived about three years after he sent the letter announcing his plan to come. For two years the apostle was under house arrest in Rome (Acts 28:30), supported at least partly by members of the churches he had planted rather than by the Christians in Rome (Philippians 1:12-18, 2:25, 4:18). Paul was probably released from this first imprisonment in Rome and may even have gotten to Spain, but some years later he was rearrested, tried, and executed in Rome.

The church in Rome

The first Christians in Rome were probably Jews.[7] They may have become Christians after Peter's first Pentecost sermon in Jerusalem (Acts 2:5, 10-11,41), or they may have heard the gospel sometime thereafter. Business, religious pilgrimage, and pleasure were constantly carrying Jews back and forth between Rome, Jerusalem, Antioch, and other cities. Some Jews probably heard the gospel in the East and carried the news back to Rome. When Paul met two Jews from Rome, Priscilla and Aquila, they were apparently already Christians (Acts 18:2-3).[8] Along with all the other Roman Jews, these two had been expelled from the capital by Emperor Claudius because of persistent rioting in the Jewish community "at the instigation of Chrestus."[9]

That expulsion took place in 49 AD, but a few years later both Christian and nonChristian Jews were back in Rome (Romans 16:3). By 57 AD there was also a substantial number of Gentile Christians in Rome, for Paul addressed both Jews and Gentiles at length in his letter (Romans 2:17, 11:11-21). Because he said a great deal about relations between Jews and Gentiles, we infer that neither group was a tiny minority in the churches.

When Paul wrote his letter, his understanding of the gospel was not the norm throughout the Empire, as it is today. A few of the Christians in Rome, such as Priscilla and Aquila, were familiar with Paul's view of the faith. However, most of the Roman Christians had been converted by other apostles' teaching. Now they were working out the details of the gospel with the Holy Spirit and the Old Testament to guide them. Some of the Roman Christians approached their relationship with Jesus from an orthodox Jewish point of view, others from an idolatrous past, and others from one of the many Jewish sects with various interpretations of the Old Testament and Jewish tradition. Paul had to keep this variety among Christians in mind as he presented his gospel as the one accurate understanding of Jesus' work. When he described how Christians should live in light of the gospel, he emphasized unity and tolerance among Christians with different gifts and customs (Romans 12:1-15:13).

The righteousness of God

Paul's letter to the Romans systematically unfolds the gospel of God's Son, the revelation of *the righteousness of God* (Romans 1:16-17). In it, Paul deals with such huge and knotty issues as sin, guilt, salvation, grace, law, faith, works, righteousness, justification, sanctification, redemption, death, resurrection, the place of the Jews in God's plan of salvation, and the way we should live in light of our salvation. Martin Luther calls this book, "the daily bread of the soul."[10] Feast on!

1. F. F. Bruce, *The Epistle to the Romans* (Grand Rapids, Michigan: William B. Eerdmans Publishing Company, 1963), page 9.
2. A. T. Robertson, "Paul, the Apostle," *The International Standard Bible Encyclopaedia,* volume 4 (Grand Rapids, Michigan: William B. Eerdmans Publishing Company, 1956), page 2276.
3. F. F. Bruce, *Paul: Apostle of the Heart Set Free* (Grand Rapids, Michigan: William B. Eerdmans Publishing Company, 1977), pages 41-43.
4. Bruce, *Paul,* pages 32-40.
5. Bruce, *Paul,* pages 50-51.
6. Bruce, *Paul,* pages 127-133.
7. Bruce, *Paul,* pages 379-382.
8. *The NIV Study Bible,* edited by Kenneth Barker (Grand Rapids, Michigan: Zondervan Corporation, 1985), page 1681.
9. Suetonius, *Life of Claudius* 25. 4. Suetonius wrote seventy years after the expulsion and apparently thought Christ was a Jew present in Rome, but the riots were probably between Christian and anti-Christian Jews. See Bruce, *Paul,* pages 381-382 for an explanation.
10. Martin Luther, *Commentary on Romans* (Grand Rapids, Michigan: Kregel Publications, 1982), page xiii.

OVERVIEW

It is much easier to study a book passage by passage if you have first examined it as a whole. An overview is especially necessary if you have never studied the book of Romans before. Below are some suggestions for an overview of Romans; do as much as you like. Look over questions 1-8 before you begin.

1. First, imagine you are one of the Roman Christians who have just received this letter from the renowned Paul. Read it through for the overall message, as you would any letter. If reading large portions of Scripture is difficult for you, try this compromise: read 1:1-17, 3:21-26, 5:1-5, 8:1-4, 9:1-5, 11:13-15, 12:1-2, 15:14-33.

2. As you read, keep a list of *repeated words and ideas* that seem important to Paul's message. This list will help you notice the main ideas Paul is trying to get across and will also suggest questions you will want to answer when you study further. For instance, you may not understand words like *justification* and *righteousness* that are central to Paul's teaching. Write your list of key words and ideas here, and note your questions under number 3 below.

_____

_____

_____

_____

_____

_____

_____

_____

_____

3. In your reading of Romans, or in the background on pages 9-14, you may have come
   across questions you'd like answered or concepts you'd like clarified. While your thoughts
   are still fresh, write your questions here. You
   can look for answers as you study further.

_____

_____

_____

_____

_____

4. Paul carefully organized his message to the
   Romans; an outline can help you trace his train
   of thought. As you read the letter, observe the
   natural breaks in Paul's thought. Then make up
   a short summary for each passage. (If you are
   reading only selections of the book, summarize
   those.)
       Here are some of the divisions the NIV
   suggests, but you can divide the book differently if you prefer:

1:1-17 _____

_____

1:18-32 _____

_____

2:1-16 _____

_____

16

2:17-3:8 _____

_____

3:9-20 _____

_____

3:21-31 _____

_____

4:1-25 _____

_____

5:1-11 _____

_____

5:12-21 _____

_____

6:1-14 _____

_____

6:15-23 _____

_____

7:1-6 _____

_____

7:7-25 _____

_____

8:1-17 _____

_____

8:18-39 _____

_____

9:1-33 _____

_____

10:1-21 _____

11:1-36 _____

12:1-21 _____

13:1-14 _____

14:1-15:13 _____

15:14-33 _____

16:1-27 _____

5. You may have noticed that 1:1-15 is basically an introduction that leads up to a statement in 1:16-17, and that the rest of the letter explains the statement in 1:16-17. Not every book of the Bible states its theme so neatly, but Paul wrote Romans more like a tight theological essay than a normal letter.

   Look back at 1:16-17 and think about what Paul says in the rest of the book. Then, in a sentence or title, state what you think is the overall message of the book of Romans.

   _____

   _____

   _____

   _____

   _____

6. There are several main divisions in the letter, several major topics Paul covers. What title would you give to each of these?

1:1-17 _____

1:18-3:20 _____
_____

3:21-4:25 (or 3:21-5:21) _____
_____

5:1-8:39 (or 6:1-8:39) _____
_____

9:1-11:36 _____
_____

12:1-15:13 _____
_____

15:14-16:27 _____

For Further Study:
Compare your answers to questions 4-6 to the outline in a study Bible or Bible handbook.

For Further Study:
For more background on Paul or the book of Romans, see a Bible dictionary or encyclopedia.

7. What do you notice about Paul as a person (his character, goals, etc.) from his letter to the Romans? If necessary, look back at 1:1-17, 9:1-5, 10:1, 11:13-14, 15:14-16:27.

_____

_____

_____

_____

_____

_____

_____

_____

8. If you have not already done so, read the background on pages 9-14. What information from there currently seems important to remember as you study Romans?

_____

_____

_____

_____

_____

_____

_____

_____

9. The last step of Bible study is applying what
you have studied to yourself. One way to make
an overview personal is to ask yourself these
questions:
> How do I want this book to affect me?
> How is the overall message of this book
relevant to my life?
> What actions or matters for prayer and
thought does my first reading of this book
encourage?
Think about these questions, and jot any
responses here.

_____

_____

_____

_____

_____

_____

For the group

This "For the group" section and the ones in later
lessons are intended to suggest ways of structuring
your discussions. Feel free to select what suits your
group.

The main goals of an introductory lesson are to
get to know the book of Romans in general and to
get to know the people with whom you are going to
study it. The group may benefit from having time to

read the "How to Use This Study" section on pages 5-8, the historical background on pages 9-14, and the whole book of Romans before everyone has to dive into detailed study.

Before group members tackle this overview, encourage them to read the whole letter but not to force themselves if they find it too difficult. Some people who are less familiar with Bible study, or less confident readers, find it frustrating to read all of a difficult book at one time. Other people have no trouble following the book at once.

Worship. Beginning with some kind of worship will help the group leave the day's concerns behind and focus on God. Some groups like to begin meetings with extended prayer and/or singing. Others prefer to start with just one song or a brief prayer for God's guidance, leaving more extensive worship until after the study.

Getting started. The beginning of a new study is a good time to lay a foundation for honest sharing of ideas, for getting comfortable with each other, and for encouraging a sense of common purpose. One way to establish common ground is to talk about what each group member hopes to get out of your group—out of your study of Romans, and out of any prayer, singing, sharing, outreach, or anything else you might do together. You can include what you each hope to give to the group as well. Why are you studying the Bible, and Romans in particular? If you have someone write down each member's hopes and expectations, then you can look back at these goals later to see if they are being met. You can then plan more time for prayer or decide to cover Romans more slowly if necessary. Also, if some people are primarily interested in studying the Bible, while others mainly want to share their lives with other Christians, all will be grateful to come to some agreement now. Suggest that each person write his or her goals in the front of this study guide for future reference.

You could take about fifteen minutes at the beginning of your discussion of lesson one to discuss goals. Or, you may prefer to take a whole meeting to introduce the study, examine the "How to Use This Study" section on pages 5-8, and share your goals.

Overview. You can structure your discussion like this:

1. *How to Use This Study.* The leader can remind the group of the main points from this section and then ask if anyone has questions about what to do. For example, point out the optional questions in the margins. These are available as group discussion questions, ideas for application, and further study. It is unlikely that anyone will have either the time or desire to answer all the optional questions and do all the applications. It is reasonable to expect a person to do *one* "Optional Application" for any given lesson. You might choose *two* "For Thought and Discussions" for your group discussion. If someone wants to write answers to the optional questions, suggest that he use a separate notebook. It will also be helpful for discussion notes, prayer requests, answers to prayers, application plans, and so on.

Note the observation-interpretation-application pattern in each lesson. Many of the numbered questions are observations and basic interpretations that lay the groundwork for deeper study. The meaty questions are often in the margins. In your group discussion, you may prefer to move quickly through the numbered questions (even skipping some) in order to concentrate on questions that interest you.

Point out the study aids on pages 209-213. If you own any, bring them in to show the group.

You may need to discuss how and why Christians memorize and meditate on Scripture. Christian meditation is not meant to empty the mind, as in oriental mysticism. Rather, after emptying your mind of distractions, you fill it with God's thoughts by dwelling on a short piece of His Word.

2. *Key words and ideas.* Ask, "What are some of the key words and ideas that struck you?"

3. *Outline.* Compare your answers for question 4 to each other and to other outlines (in your study Bibles, Bible dictionaries, the outlines on page 24, etc.). For example, let each person answer, "What is 1:18-32 about?" Then compare answers to question 6. Discuss the merits of different outlines. You'll find quite a variety of approaches if you look at several commentaries and dictionaries. You may want to evaluate different outlines again when you review the book after studying in detail.

4. *Theme.* What is the book about? Why did

Paul write to the Romans? (The background on pages 9-14 may help with this.) What does 1:16-17 tell you about Paul's theme?

5. *Paul.* It will be easier to apply Paul's words to yourselves if you see him as a real person with real feelings and goals. What does this letter reveal about him? What does the background on pages 9-14 add?

6. *The Romans.* What do you know from the background and the letter about Paul's readers? (Also, why is it important to know something about them?)

7. *Questions.* Record any questions group members have about the book. You may not want to answer them now, but you can all look for answers as you go along and discuss them at the appropriate times.

8. *Application.* If your group is not already familiar with how to apply Scripture to your lives, think of some sample ways of putting Paul's teaching into practice. Choose a paragraph from Romans, decide what it means, define the truth that is relevant to your lives, and think of one practical way in which you could act on that truth. This might include prayer, talking to someone, or doing something.

Wrap-up. The wrap-up is a time to bring the discussion to a focused end and to make any announcements about the next lesson or meeting. For example, you might ask the group to look at the box labeled "Study Skill—Application" on page 31 before beginning the questions in lesson two. Then members can be looking for ways to apply the passage as they study it.

Some people tend to prepare lessons for group discussions only one or two days before the meetings and then feel that it is too late to start working on an application. Tell the group that it is alright to begin memorizing a verse or thinking about an application after the group discussion of that passage.

Worship. Thank God for the book of Romans. Praise Him for some particular things He has revealed to you about Himself through this book. Ask Him to enable you each to understand and apply His words in this letter.

Outlines. Here are two of many possible ways to outline Romans:[1]

I. Introduction (1:1-15)
II. Theme: Righteousness from God (1:16-17)
III. The Unrighteousness of All Mankind (1:18-3:20)
    A. Gentiles (1:18-32)
    B. Jews (2:1-3:8)
    C. Summary: All people (3:9-20)
IV. Righteousness Imputed: Justification (3:21-5:21)
V. Righteousness Imparted: Sanctification (6:1-8:39)
VI. God's Righteousness Vindicated: The Problem of the Rejection of Israel (9:1-11:32)
VII. Righteousness Practiced (12:1-15:13)
VIII. Conclusion (15:14-33)
IX. Commendation and Greetings (16:1-27)

I. Superscription, Address and Salutation (1:1-7)
II. Paul and the Roman Church (1:8-16a)
III. The Theme of the Epistle Stated (1:16b-17)
IV. The Revelation of the Righteousness which is from God by Faith Alone—"He who is righteous by faith" expounded (1:18-4:25)
V. The Life Promised for Those who are Righteous by Faith—"Shall live" expounded (5:1-8:39)
VI. The Unbelief of Men and the Faithfulness of God (9:1-11:36)
VII. The Obedience to which Those who are Righteous by Faith are Called (12:1-15:13)
VIII. Conclusion to the Epistle (15:14-16:27)

1. The first is from *The NIV Study Bible*, pages 1704-1705; the second is from C.E.B. Cranfield, *Romans: A Shorter Commentary* (Grand Rapids, Michigan: William B. Eerdmans Publishing Company, 1985), pages xv-xvii.

ROMANS 1:1-17

Introduction

Paul knew only some of the Christians in Rome (16:1-16). Could he expect people he had never met to provide him with a headquarters and funds for his mission to Western Europe? Possibly yes, if he could convince them of the urgency of the mission and his own qualifications to lead it.

Read 1:1-17, asking God to show you what is important in this introduction to the letter.

Greeting (1:1-7)

Servant (1:1). In the Old Testament, a servant of God was a high official in the Lord's royal administration, such as Moses, Samuel, David, and the mysterious messianic "Servant" (Isaiah 42:1-7).[1] To the Gentile mind, a servant was either a freeman who chose to work for his master or a slave who utterly belonged to his master and was not free to leave. All these ideas are probably included in Paul's intent.

Apostle (1:1). Literally, "one who is sent"—a messenger, proxy, ambassador. In Jewish law, this was the *shaliach*, "a person acting with full authority for another" in a business or legal transaction.[2]

The early Church recognized certain men who had seen the risen Jesus as apostles—the leaders with highest authority regarding

For Thought and
Discussion: a. Why
is it important for you
to know what 1:2-4
says about Jesus?
What difference do
these verses make to
your life?
   b. What errors
about Jesus do these
verses refute?

doctrine and policy. Twelve of Jesus' original
disciples (Luke 6:12-16, Acts 1:12-26) and Paul
had this honor. Barnabas (Acts 14:14), James
the brother of Jesus (Galatians 1:19) and perhaps Andronicus and Junias (Romans 16:7) are
also called apostles, but possibly in a wider
sense of "messenger."[3]

1. Paul expanded on the customary beginning of a
   letter to identify himself and his mission to
   people who did not know him. In 1:1-7, how
   does Paul identify . . .

   himself (1:1)? _____

   _____

   _____

   _____

   his message (1:2-4)? _____

   _____

   _____

   _____

   his mission (1:5)? _____

   _____

   _____

   _____

   his readers (1:6-7)? _____

   _____

   _____

   _____

   _____

Gospel (1:1). The Old English word *godspel* means
   "good news." It translates the Greek word
   euangelion (*eu-*, "good" and *angelion*, "mes-

26

sage"), which also gives us words like "evangelist" and "angel."

Obedience that comes from faith (1:5). Literally, "the obedience of faith." Some interpreters think Paul means the practical obedience that comes from believing in Jesus, while others think he means that faith itself, rather than law-keeping, is the true obedience God desires.[4]

Saints (1:7). "Saint," "sanctify," and "holiness" all refer to the same Greek word-group that means "set apart," as in 1:1. Thus, a saint is a "holy one" or "set apart one." A saint is already set apart for God and in the process of being made holy by the Holy Spirit.

---

2. Like the Romans, we too have been called to the obedience of faith and to be saints/ holy/set apart (1:5-6). What are some actions, decisions, and priorities this calling implies for your life?

_____

_____

_____

_____

_____

_____

_____

Study Skill—Repetition
Repetition is a clue to the ideas an author wants to emphasize. Observe the words Paul repeats in 1:1-7—*Lord, Jesus, Christ, God, Son, apostle(ship), gospel, call(ed), set apart/holiness/saints, grace*. Notice that Paul applies being "called" and "set apart" for "Christ Jesus" to his own life (1:1-5) and then to the Romans' lives (1:6-7).
(continued on page 28)

For Thought and Discussion: a. In what sense is faith itself an aspect of obedience?

b. Why does true faith also lead to obedience?

Optional Application: What have you been set apart to be and do? What have you been set apart from? How can you fulfill this holy status better?

For Further Study: The words "call" and "called" recur four times in 1:1-7. Who calls? Who are called? What are they called to be and do?

For Thought and Discussion: How do we know that Jesus is the Son of God (1:4)?

(continued from page 27)

Optional Application: Read the section called "Memorizing and Meditating" on page 7. For a few minutes each day for the next several days, meditate on:

who Jesus is (1:3-4);

who you are (1:6); or

the obedience of faith (1:5).
Look for implications for your life that you could act upon.

Optional Application: To what extent do you have the same mission Paul does (1:5)? How can you practice it better?

Look for repetition in later passages as clues to Paul's main point. For instance, the word *righteousness* occurs about thirty times. You will also find *justify(ed), faith, works, law, grace, sin, flesh, spirit,* and *slavery* appearing frequently.

Grace (1:5,7). God's unmerited favor and gifts to humanity. Later in Romans, Paul will write at length about how we are justified by the gracious gift of God's Son. Here, however, Paul is talking about God's daily gift of ability to live the Christian life and fulfill our missions.

Grace (Greek: *charis*) resembles the typical Greek greeting, *charein* ("favor from me to you").

Peace (1:7). The usual Jewish greeting in letters. It referred to the wholeness and well-being in all relationships (social harmony, physical health, nearness to God) that would be true in the Messianic Age because of God's presence among His people. Paul will say more about both grace and peace later in his letter.

Paul's plan (1:8-15)

It was common to follow a letter's greeting with thanks for the reader's welfare and prayer that it may continue. Paul adapts this custom for a Christian purpose.

3. For what does Paul thank God (1:8)?

_____

_____

_____

_____

4. What does Paul pray for (1:9-10)?

_____

_____

_____

_____

_____

5. Why does Paul want to go to Rome (1:11-15)?

_____

_____

_____

_____

_____

Paul's theme (1:16-17)

_____

Salvation (1:16). Stated negatively, it is deliverance from every evil, particularly sin, death, and rejection from God's presence. Stated positively, it is spiritual and physical healing, the bestowal of all blessings.[5]

Righteousness from God (1:17). The state of being "in the right" or declared "not guilty" in relationship to God. This is a legal term.

By faith (1:17). Literally, "from faith to faith." This might mean, "by faith from first to last."

6. Why is Paul unashamed to preach the gospel, even among strangers in a sophisticated place like Rome or a foreign place like Spain (1:16)?

_____

_____

_____

_____

_____

For Thought and Discussion: What character qualities and priorities does Paul show in 1:1-17? What kind of person does he seem to be?

Optional Application: In what ways would you like to be more like Paul? Talk to God about how this can happen. Plan what you can do and what you must rely on God to do. Persistently ask God to keep doing His part and to enable you to do yours.

Optional Application: Thank God for revealing His way of righteousness. Ask Him to help you fully understand and obey it

Optional Application: Do you ever feel or act ashamed of the gospel? Why? If you do, confess and meditate on 1:16-17. Ask God to really convince you that the gospel is His power to save.

For Thought and Discussion: In what ways is the gospel good news (1:2-7,16-17)?

For Further Study: On some blank paper or on the blank pages at the end of this study guide, begin an outline of Romans. Use as much detail as you like.

7. How does the gospel enable people to be saved (1:17)?

_____

_____

_____

_____

_____

8. In what ways are Paul's priorities, attitudes, and desires in 1:1-17 good examples for you to follow?

_____

_____

_____

_____

_____

Your response

Study Skill—Outlining

You made a rough outline of the whole book of Romans in your overview. You can do the same thing with each passage. If you do this as you go along or at the end of your study, you will have a clearer picture of Paul's train of thought.

For example, you can think about the repeated words in 1:1-17, then briefly outline what Paul says. If your Bible marks paragraphs, you can simply give a title to each one, like this:

    I. Introduction (1:1-17)
       A. Greeting: Called One to Called Ones (1:1-7)
       B. Paul's Plan: To Visit Rome (1:8-15)
       C. Paul's Theme: The Righteousness of God (1:16-17)

9. Paul states the theme of his letter in 1:17. Look at that verse, and write down at least two questions you hope he will answer in the rest of his letter in connection with this theme.

_____

_____

_____

_____

_____

_____

Optional Application: This week, find one way to act in the obedience of faith because you are righteous by faith and living by faith.

Optional Application: Meditate on your calling (1:5-7). How can you live out your calling this week?

Study Skill—Application

James 1:22 urges us to do what the Word says, not merely hear it. Therefore, the last step of Bible study is asking ourselves, "What difference should this passage make to my life? How should it make me want to think or act?" Application will require time, thought, prayer, and perhaps even discussion with another person.

At times, you may find it most productive to concentrate on one specific application, giving it careful thought and prayer. At other times you may want to list many implications a passage of Scripture has for your life, and then choose one to concentrate on for prayer and action. Use whatever method helps you to grow more obedient to God's Word.

Some possible ways to approach application are: "I will pray about . . . consistently for the next week, asking for ability, guidance, and discipline to obey by God's strength." "I want to stop . . . , and my first step will be . . . ." "I will ask the Holy Spirit to help me to . . . ." "I will thank God for . . . ." "I will start . . . ."

10. What insight from 1:1-17 seems most applicable to you right now?

_____

_____

31

_____

_____

_____

11. How would you like that insight to affect your life?

_____

_____

_____

_____

_____

12. What prayer and other action can you pursue this week to respond to that insight?

_____

_____

_____

_____

_____

13. List any questions you have about 1:1-17.

_____

_____

_____

_____

_____

For the group

Warm-up. A simple question that deals generally with the topic of the study but focuses on people's experience can help the group shift from the day's affairs to Bible study. You needn't even discuss the warm-up question; you can just think about it for a minute in silence. A possible warm-up for this lesson is, "Think of one time in the past few days when you had to act in faith in God." Another possibility is, "How did God first call you to belong to Jesus Christ?" Questions like these help a group get to know each other.

Read aloud. Even when the group has studied the passage ahead of time, most people will be glad to have their memories refreshed. So, have someone read 1:1-17 aloud.

Summarize. A quick summary at the outset helps to set the context for the rest of the discussion. Ask someone to tell briefly what 1:1-17 is about. This need not be the best possible summary, since you will summarize the passage again after discussing it in detail.

Questions. Questions 1 and 4-7 are relatively simple observation questions, so you should be able to cover them quickly. If you have time, discuss one or two of the "For Thought and Discussions" that interest you. However, try to spend at least half of your discussion time on application questions like 2, 8, and 10-12. Think of as many general and specific personal implications of this passage as you can. Let anyone share what he or she has learned about his or her calling, faith, righteousness, sainthood, etc.

Question 9 should raise some questions that you will want to answer as you go along. For instance:

> How is the gospel God's power for salvation?
> What do we need to believe in order to receive this salvation?
> Why is salvation for the Jew first?
> What is the righteousness from God that is revealed?
> What does it mean that this righteousness is "by faith"?
> Why is it by faith?

If the members of your group do not know each other well, they may be reluctant to share applications that are deeply personal. One of the benefits of group study is the support you can give each other as you seek to grow in faith and holiness, but you cannot force premature intimacy. If you sense reserve on the part of some or all group members, set an example by openly sharing some of the ways you are applying the passage. Also, make an effort outside of the discussion of the passage to foster trust and frankness among members. You could plan time at the beginning of your next meeting to share something about your backgrounds with each other. Warm-up questions can help with this. Or, you could plan time together away from the study. Try anything that will make your group a place for more than just academic discussion.

Give everyone a chance to share his or her own questions about the passage (question 13). Encourage the group, rather than the leader, to answer any questions that can be answered from the passage. Write down any questions that can be answered later from Romans, so that you can come back to those questions at the end of your study.

Summarize. This is a fairly easy passage to summarize, so your summary may be almost the same now as at the beginning. However, when you get to the more difficult parts of Romans, you may be much better able to summarize after your discussions.

Wrap-up.

Worship. Thank God for the gospel of His Son that is powerful to save. Thank Him for anything else in 1:1-17 and for what He is doing in your lives.

1. Roland de Vaux, *Ancient Israel: Volume 1: Social Institutions* (New York: McGraw-Hill Book Company, 1961), page 80; *The NIV Study Bible,* pages 108, 1074, 1076.
2. Erich von Eicken and Helgo Lindner, "Apostle," *The New International Dictionary of New Testament Theology,* volume 1, edited by Colin Brown (Grand Rapids, Michigan: Zondervan Corporation, 1975), page 128.
3. *The NIV Study Bible,* page 1505.
4. Cranfield, page 8.
5. Colin Brown, "Sozo," *The New International Dictionary of New Testament Theology,* volume 3 (1978), pages 205-213.

ROMANS 1:18-32

The Wrath of God

"In the gospel," says Paul, "a righteousness from God is revealed" (1:17). Why is this way to rightness with God crucial? Paul begins his explanation by describing something else that is being revealed all around his readers. Christians in the first or twentieth century need only to walk the streets to see the condition into which humanity has fallen.

As you read 1:18-32, think about your own society.

Study Skill—Making Connections

As you go deeper into Paul's letter, it will be important to keep track of how each passage relates to the one before and to Paul's theme—the righteousness of God. The paragraph above suggests a way of relating 1:18-32 to the theme.

In later lessons, you will be making these connections yourself. Two questions to bear in mind are:

1. What overall point is Paul making in this passage?
2. What does this have to do with what comes before (and after)?[1]

The outline on pages 16-18, or one in your Bible handbook or study Bible, may help you make these connections. Glance at an outline before you study each passage.

---

1. What is Paul's overall point in 1:18-32?

_____

_____

_____

_____

_____

2. Paul says that man's wickedness suppresses the truth (1:18). What truth are people suppressing (1:19-20)?

_____

_____

_____

_____

3. How have they suppressed that truth?

what they don't do (1:21) _____

_____

_____

_____

what they do instead (1:22-23,25) _____

_____

_____

_____

_____

4. The decision to suppress the truth has had many effects upon mankind. What results does Paul name in 1:24-32?

1:24 _____

_____

1:26-27 _____

_____

1:28-31 _____

_____

_____

1:32 _____

_____

5. The overarching result of suppressing the truth and the root of all the sins in 1:24-32 is *futile thinking* and *a darkened heart* (1:21). Reflect on one of your habitual faults. How is it rooted in futile thinking?

_____

_____

_____

_____

_____

6. Why would someone consider it unworthwhile to retain the knowledge of God (1:28)?

_____

_____

_____

_____

_____

_____

7. In light of 1:18,21,28, what needs to change in a person before he or she can understand the gospel and forsake sin?

_____

_____

For Thought and Discussion: Why is God angry at wickedness (1:18)? Does this contradict His nature as a loving God? Why or why not?

For Thought and Discussion: Name some ways in which the created world reveals God's eternal power and divinity (1:20).

Optional Application: a. Why does God deserve the two responses that wicked people omit (1:21)?
b. How can you make these two responses a priority in your life this week?

For Thought and Discussion: Why does disobedience to parents (1:30) belong in this catalog of vices?

Optional Application: Does any of Paul's list of vices suggest an area in which you need to repent? Consider greed, envy, strife, deceit, boastfulness, disobedience, etc. (1:24-32).

For Thought and Discussion: What does it mean that God "gave them over" to depravity?

Optional Application: How can your answers to questions 6 and 7 affect the way you evangelize and pray for people?

For Thought and Discussion: To what extent does 1:18-32 describe the world around you and your own life before you committed yourself to Christ?

8. Why does God give people over (1:24,26,28) to depraved minds and actions? In view of 1:21-23,28, why is this just?

9. What loving ends could giving people over to depravity serve? (*Optional:* See Ezekiel 20:25-26,39,43-44; Amos 4:6-11.)

Your response

In 1:18-32, Paul has depicted a certain kind of person against whom God's wrath is revealed. We could call him or her the wicked or immoral person. To summarize this passage, you could describe what the immoral person is and does. For application, you could compare yourself to that description and see where you need to repent.

However, we will take the reverse approach. Read back through 1:18-32, and in the chart on the next page list characteristics that are the *opposite* of those Paul is condemning. You will then have a description of the holy person God desires. For application, you can measure yourself by this positive standard.

10. The Holy Opposite of the Immoral Person
in 1:18-32
_____

11. Circle one of the characteristics you just named.
Confess to God any ways in which you fall short
of this standard. Ask His forgiveness. Ask Him
to enable you to become more holy in this area.
Ask Him what actions and persistent prayer you
can pursue to begin living this godly trait. Write
your plans here and on the next page.

_____

_____

For Further Study:
Make up your own
outline of 1:18-32,
and add it to your out-
line of 1:1-11. Try to
show how 1:18-32
relates to the theme
in 1:16-17.

_____

_____

_____

_____

12. If you have any questions about 1:18-32, list
them.

_____

_____

_____

_____

For the group

Warm-up. Here are two possible warm-up exercises:
1. Name one way in which you have seen God's
power and divinity evident in your world during the
past week.
2. Name one reason you have had to give
thanks to God this week.

Read aloud.

Summarize. What is 1:18-32 about? How does it fit
into Paul's theme: the gospel of righteousness from
God?

Questions. You should be able to move quickly
through the observation questions (2-4) and spend
more time on interpretation (5-10) and application
(5, 11). Cover as many of the optional questions as
you like. Most of these deal with issues we encounter when we try to explain the gospel to nonChristians. Some are questions people ask: "How can God
be both angry and loving?" Others are truths we
need to know to share the gospel properly: "What is
the real barrier between people and God?"
      The group may find it easier to apply 1:18-32 if
you discuss ways in which the passage describes
your (past or present) selves and the world around
you. (How do people today suppress the truth about
God? Do they glorify and thank Him? In what ways

40

is their thinking futile? How do they worship created things? How common are the vices of 1:29-32?)

Most of us retain some of these sinful habits and attitudes toward God to some degree. We resist giving thanks, our minds are not fully enlightened, and so on. Take time at the end of your meeting to pray for each other and for people you know to fully abandon all of these sins.

Hopefully, the group has read all of Paul's letter and knows what the denunciation of 1:18-32 is leading to. However, when you discuss how you will apply 1:18-32 to your lives, remind the group that if you have faith in Christ you are forgiven for any sinful habits you still have, and the Spirit of God is available to change you (8:1-39). So, you are free to ask God to help you abandon any of the sins in 1:18-32. If necessary, read 1 John 1:8-10 to the group, then ask what a Christian can do if he or she has been convicted by Romans 1:18-32.

1. Fee and Stuart, pages 51-52.

ROMANS 2:1-29

God's Standards

When you studied 1:18-32, were you tempted to point the finger at the world around you? Paul's Roman readers would have thought first of their Gentile neighbors—heathens, pagans, unbelievers. A "good" Jew or "moral" Gentile might have applauded God's wrath upon such people. But Paul wanted no one to imagine that God's wrath and God's righteousness by faith are only for some especially bad sinners. Paul addressed 2:1-29 particularly to his fellow Jews, who tended to look down on Gentiles for their idolatry and loose morals. But the passage applies equally to self-righteous Gentiles.

Read 2:1-29 for its overall message and its connection with 1:16-32.

God's impartiality (2:1-16)

1. In your initial reading, what main point does Paul seem to be making in 2:1-16?

_____

_____

_____

_____

_____

_____

43

Study Skill—Connecting Words

Connecting words are clues to the logic in a passage. Connectives may show:

Time: *after, as, before, then, until, when, while;*

Place: *in, where;*

Conclusion or Result: *so, then, therefore, thus;*

Purpose: *in order that, so that;*

Cause: *because, for, since;*

Contrast: *although, but, much more, nevertheless, otherwise, yet;*

Comparison: *also, as, as . . . so, just as . . . so, likewise, so also;*

Source: *by means of, from, through;*

Series of Points: *and, first of all, lastly, or.*

For example, the word *therefore* in 2:1 shows the connection between 2:1-16 and 1:18-32. Because wicked people know they should honor and obey God, know they are doing wrong, and know the penalty for wrongdoing, they are without excuse (1:20,32). *Therefore,* you who do the same things are also without excuse (2:1).

Use connecting words to follow Paul's logic in later passages.

Pass judgment (2:1). Jesus and Paul both urge us to discern when someone's teaching or behavior is ungodly (Matthew 7:15-20, 2 Timothy 2:23-4:5). We may even rebuke a sinner gently, if necessary (Luke 17:3-4, Galatians 6:1), with a loving eye to repentance, but all feelings of scorn, superiority, condescension, or self-righteousness are to be confessed as sin before we confront the person (Matthew 7:1-5).

2. What do people deserve if they do the things God hates (1:32, 2:2)?

_____

_____

3. Has God withheld the just consequences of any sins you have committed recently? If so, why has He done this (2:4)?

_____

_____

_____

_____

4. Therefore, why should you *not* judge other people's sin (2:1-4)?

_____

_____

_____

_____

_____

Law (2:12). The Law of Moses. Most Jews were proud of knowing God's Word and despised Gentiles who did not know it (2:17-20). Many Jews believed that God would give them eternal life just because they were born into Jewish families or because they knew God's Word.

It was extremely hard for Jews and Gentiles to overcome their prejudices enough to live and worship together as Christians.

5. By what standards does God judge . . .

Jews (or Christians), who know God's Law (2:6-13)?

_____

_____

_____

_____

For Thought and Discussion: How have you experienced God's patience and kindness toward sinners?

Optional Application: a. Have you judged anyone for sin in the past week? If so, why?
b. Ask God to change your attitude. Memorize 2:1 or 2:4.

For Further Study: What are some guidelines we can follow when we think something is wrong with another Christian's life? See Matthew 5:23-24, 18:15-20; Galatians 6:1-5; Hebrews 3:12-13.

For Thought and Discussion: Some modern people believe they are saved because their families are Christian, because they go to church, or because they know the Bible. By what standard will God judge such people (2:5-11)?

45

For Thought and Discussion: a. If it were possible to obey God's Law on your own, without His enabling power, would God declare you righteous without faith in Christ's work (2:13)? Why or why not?

b. Does anyone in fact live up even to the moral law common to all people (1:21,28; 3:10-11)?

Gentiles, who do not know God's Law (2:6-12)?

_____

_____

_____

_____

6. What future reward or punishment do God's standards suggest you personally deserve (2:9-10)?

_____

_____

_____

_____

Declared righteous (2:13). "Justified" in RSV, KJV, and NASB. On the Judgment Day, God will pronounce obedient people legally "not guilty" of the charges against them and "in the right" before Him. Righteousness or justification (the same word in Greek) is essentially a legal concept. Watch for it in the rest of Paul's letter.

When Gentiles, who do not have the law . . . (2:14-16). Paul is giving an example of people who do what the Law says, even though they have not been brought up with it as Jews. At least two interpretations have been offered for these verses:

1. Gentile pagans sometimes do what God's Law requires in obedience to an innate or learned moral law inside them. On Judgment Day, their consciences will witness to both the good and the bad they have done according to the law they know. Of course, even the best people will turn out to fall short of the law within them, but they will be judged by that standard.

2. Gentile Christian converts now have God's Law on their hearts (Jeremiah 31:33, Romans 2:15), although they do not have the

46

Law by upbringing. On Judgment Day, their consciences will witness that although they have fallen short in every area, their deeds have begun to show the fruit of their faith in Christ. God will justify them because of their faith in Jesus, demonstrated by deeds done by His strength for His glory.[1]

Optional Application: What key truths in 2:1-16 are relevant to the gospel you share with unbelievers? Make a list of them.

Applied to the Jews (2:17-29)

Now Paul applies God's standard explicitly to the Jews, who were often inclined to judge their neighbors and feel self-righteous. Think about to what extent you are ever like these Jews.

7. Why did some Jews think God considered them superior to Gentiles (2:17-20)?

_____

_____

_____

_____

_____

_____

Rob temples (2:22). Quantities of wealth were often kept in pagan temples. The town clerk of Ephesus defended Paul by pointing out that this Jew had not robbed any temples (Acts 19:37), so some people have inferred that Jews actually did this.[2] God's Law commanded Israel to destroy pagan temples in Canaan (Deuteronomy 7:1-6), and zealous Jews sometimes acted on this statute. They often broke the Law by confiscating the temples' treasures (Deuteronomy 20:16-18; Joshua 6:18-19; 7:1,20).

8. How did the Jews prove that they were not superior to the Gentiles (2:21-24)?

47

For Thought and Discussion: a. How are Christians sometimes guilty of what 2:23-24 describes?

b. Do you know any Christians who brag about their relationship to God or knowledge of His Word (2:17-20)? What does 2:17-24 have to say to such people?

Optional Application: Confess any ways in which 2:17-24 describes you. Ask God to change your attitudes and show you when you fall in this area this week. Meditate daily on 2:17-24 and memorize at least one verse.

Optional Application: Ask God to circumcise your heart by the Spirit (2:29), and meditate on what that means. Think of one practical way you can act on this inner circumcision.

9. Are Christians today ever like the Jews Paul describes in 2:17-24? If so, what is Paul's message to us?

_____

_____

_____

_____

_____

_____

Circumcision (2:25). A ritual cutting away of the foreskin, which signified that a man was a Jew. It was supposed to demonstrate that a man had committed himself to obey the Lord; it invited God to cut off the man and his heirs if he rebelled against God (Genesis 17:14).[3] However, many Jews came to think that the mere rite guaranteed their membership among God's people. Moses and the prophets warned Israel that the ritual was meaningless unless it accompanied "circumcision of the heart" (Deuteronomy 10:16, 30:6; Jeremiah 4:4).

Those who are not circumcised (2:26-27). As in 2:14-15, Paul has in mind here either:

1. Gentile pagans who do what the Law requires. (But how can they do it enough to be regarded as circumcised?)

2. Gentile Christians who obey God but are not circumcised. (In Paul's day, there were still many Jewish Christians who thought that faith in Christ was not alone sufficient to assure God's justification. They believed that a convert also had to keep the Jewish ritual law, including circumcision.)

48

10. According to Romans 2:25-29, what is circumcision of the heart, and how is it demonstrated?

_____

_____

_____

_____

_____

_____

11. Paul's purpose in Romans 2 is to answer these questions: "Of course those Gentile pagans are scum (1:18-32), but what about us who know God's Word? Aren't we free from God's wrathful judgment?" Summarize how Paul answers in 2:1-29.

_____

_____

_____

_____

_____

_____

12. In lesson three, you described the opposite of the immoral person. Now, reread 2:1-4,17-29 and list characteristics of the person who is *not* self-righteous.

The Holy Person Who Is Not Self-Righteous
_____

Optional Application: In what ways do you seek praise from men, and in what ways from God (2:29)? How would seeking praise only from God affect your actions at home or work? Think of at least one specific way, and act on it.

For Thought and Discussion: What can we learn about God from Romans 2?

For Further Study: Outline 2:1-29. Try to show how it is connected to 1:18-32.

49

13. Confess any ways in which you have fallen short of this standard. Ask God's forgiveness. What action can you take this week to practice what you described in question 12?

_____

_____

_____

_____

_____

_____

14. List any questions you have about chapter 2.

_____

_____

_____

_____

For the group

Warm-up. A possible question is: "Does your behavior give unbelievers a reason to honor or to reject God? How?"

Read aloud.

Summarize.

God's impartiality. Focus on what 2:1-16 can tell us about 1) God's character and standards, 2) how we measure up to those standards, and 3) what our attitudes and actions should be because of (1) and (2).

Some of the specifics of this passage are open to debate, such as 2:14-16. Avoid a long argument about which of the two interpretations on pages 46-47 is correct. Center instead on the main issues, and look for specific applications.

Never feel you must answer all of the questions in a lesson. You can have someone explain Paul's argument briefly and then move on to optional questions and applications. If your group is familiar with the gospel, members may find the observation questions less interesting than the deeper questions in the margins. Encourage each person to treat this study guide flexibly and to explore whatever interests him or her. Choose discussion questions from the numbered and marginal ones to suit your group.

Applied to the Jews. Almost any passage can be systematically studied if you use this framework:

> context (How does 2:17-29 relate to 2:1-16?)
> observe (What does Paul say about wrong Jewish attitudes and right attitudes?)
> interpret (What do particular sentences mean?)
> apply (How are you like the Jews Paul rebukes? How can you acquire more perfectly the attitudes and habits he urges?)
> summarize (What is the overall point of 2:17-29?)

Growing together. By your third or fourth meeting you may know each other well enough to share the weaknesses you perceive in yourselves. Your partnership as a group (Philippians 1:5) should include trusting each other and being worthy of that trust. It also includes sharing responsibility to pray for and encourage each other. As you reveal desires, efforts, successes, and failures, you give one another chances to practice love, humility, acceptance, and concern for others. You can learn from each other how to grow in character by God's grace, and how to respond when you fail. Urge the group to take these responsibilities seriously. As the group leader, you can set an example by sharing how you would like to grow more forgiving of others' faults (for instance) and what you intend to do about it.

Summarize.

Wrap-up. Because lesson five is long, you may decide to divide it and cover it in two weeks. Plan ahead if you want to do this.

Worship. Think of things you learned about God in chapter 2, and praise Him for them. Thank Him for what He's done for each of you this week.

The Law

By what "law" will God measure men's deeds (2:6,12-15)? Jesus gives us some clues. In Luke 18:18-27, a man asks Jesus how to inherit eternal life, and Jesus lists several of the Ten Commandments in response (Exodus 20:1-17). The inquirer fails the test when he refuses to give up the possessions he covets and follow Jesus as his Lord (compare Exodus 20:1-3,17). But Jesus hints that there is hope even for this failure (Luke 18:24-27).

Also, in Luke 10:25-28, another man asks Jesus the same question. This time, Jesus directs the man to the two great Old Testament laws—love God and love your neighbor (Deuteronomy 6:5, Leviticus 19:18). The instruction to the other man was similar: love God (follow Jesus) and love your neighbor as yourself (give your possessions to the poor). "All the Law and the Prophets [the whole Old Testament] hang on these two commandments," says Jesus (Matthew 22:40). Paul restates this very principle in Romans 13:8-10. In John 13:34-35 and 15:12-14, Jesus deepens the law of love: Demonstrate your love for Me by loving others *beyond* your love for self.

---

1. Cranfield, pages 50-54.
2. John Murray, *The Epistle to the Romans,* (Grand Rapids, Michigan: William B. Eerdmans Publishing Company, 1959), pages 83-84.
3. *The NIV Study Bible,* page 31.

ROMANS 3:1-31

Bad News/Good News

Romans 1:18-2:29 has been grim, and Paul isn't finished with indictment. We have to face the bad news before we can grasp the magnitude of the good news. Read 3:1-31 prayerfully. Glance at the outlines on page 24 if you find they help you orient yourself.

Objections (3:1-8)

Paul has exposed the sinfulness of the mass of humanity (1:18-32). God judges both Jews and Gentiles by their deeds, impartially (2:1-16). If a Jew breaks God's Law, he is as bad as a wicked uncircumcised Gentile and worse than a Gentile who obeys God (2:17-29). Against such sin, "the wrath of God is being revealed" (1:18). A Jew might object to the way Paul puts him on an equal level with pagans. "What advantage, then, is there in being a Jew . . ." (3:1) if it doesn't guarantee salvation? "Much," says Paul, for the Jews have "the very words of God" (3:2)—the Scriptures.

1. In what ways is it an advantage to know God's revelation of Himself, His promises, His deeds, and His guidance for living? (*Optional:* See Deuteronomy 4:5-8, Psalm 19:7-11.)

   _____

   _____

   _____

For Thought and
Discussion: What
advantages and
responsibilities do
Christians have in
comparison to
nonChristians?

Optional
Application: How
can you better fulfill
the responsibilities
you have because you
know God's Word?

For Thought and
Discussion: How has
God shown His faith-
fulness to His prom-
ises to save the world
through the Jews, pro-
tect them, and disci-
pline them?

2. What responsibilities go along with being
entrusted with God's words? (*Optional:* See
Isaiah 43:10-13, Amos 3:2, Luke 12:47-48, John
14:21, Romans 2:12-13.)

3. What implications does this have for Christians
(and you personally), who have even more of
God's words than the Jews had?

God's faithfulness (3:3). God promised that He
would be Israel's God, remain with and protect
His people, and send the Savior of the world
through them. He also promised to punish His
people if they disobeyed Him, so that they
would learn to obey. These promises remain
valid, even though many Jews have rebelled
against God and rejected His way of righteousness. God has kept His covenant; it is man who
has faltered. Paul treats the topic of God's faithfulness and the Jews' unbelief more fully in
9:1-11:32.

54

So that you may be proved right . . . (3:4). God's judgment upon man's faithlessness (disloyalty, lying, sin) proves God's faithfulness to His righteous character and covenant promises.

But if . . . (3:5). Romans 3:4 leads to a second objection that either a Jew or a Gentile might raise: If man's faithlessness, falsehood, and sin contrast and enhance God's faithfulness, truth, and righteousness, then man's sin glorifies God. Therefore, the wrath of 1:18 and 2:8 is unjust (3:5), and sinners shouldn't be punished (3:7). Paul scarcely bothers to refute this nonsense. God is the Creator of earth and man, the Inventor of our consciences, and the Definer of right and wrong. If He doesn't have the right to judge, then no one does and morality is meaningless (3:6).

Let us do evil . . . (3:8). Some people believed that Paul's doctrine of justification by grace would lead people to sin, so that God would give more of His grace to mankind. Paul refutes this distortion thoroughly in chapter 6; here he merely rejects it as absurd.

Conclusion (3:9-20)

4. Jews have at least one advantage over Gentiles: they have been entrusted with God's words (3:1). However, in the final analysis, why are Jews and Gentiles essentially equal (3:9)?

_____

_____

_____

_____

Study Skill—Old Testament Quotations
Romans 3:4 and 3:10-18 are just two of the many places in which Paul quotes the Old Testament. If you compare those quotations
(continued on page 56)

For Thought and Discussion: a. Do you or anyone you know ever feel that God has no right to judge the world or that He is unfair or breaks His promises? If so, how can 3:1-8 help you see God more clearly?

b. How does 1:18-2:29 help you see why God's judgment is just?

Optional Application: Meditate on God's faithfulness and justice in judging sin (3:3-7). If necessary, ask Him to help you believe He is fair and loving.

Optional Application: Read 3:9-18 meditatively, asking God to show you how you commit any of those sins. If you are convicted, confess and ask for help to turn from those sins.

Optional Application: Take time tomorrow to read the Ten Commandments (Exodus 20:1-17) thoughtfully. Ask God to make you conscious of your sin through the Law, as Romans 3:20 says. Confess and ask for mercy and the grace to change.

For Thought and Discussion: How does Paul use the repeated words "no one" and "all" in 3:9-18 to make his point?

(continued from page 55)
with the original, you will notice differences for several reasons:

    1. New Testament writers often give "the general sense" of a passage rather than quoting it word-for-word.

    2. They often quote from the *Septuagint*, the Greek translation of the Old Testament which was used by many Jews and all Gentiles.

    3. A New Testament writer sometimes enlarges, abbreviates, or adapts an Old Testament passage, or combines two or more passages to make his point. The Holy Spirit has inspired these adaptations just as He has inspired the rest of the New Testament.[1]

Law (3:19). The whole Old Testament. In 3:10-18, Paul quotes from the Psalms, Ecclesiastes, and Isaiah, not the books of Moses.

    Paul uses the word *law* flexibly in Romans, so we have to interpret him according to the context. For example, in 3:27 NIV and RSV sometimes render the word *law* as "principle." NASB and KJV have the literal "law of faith."

---

5. What are some purposes of God's Law (3:19-20)?

_____

_____

_____

Study Skill—Think Paragraphs
Paul's logic is sometimes easiest to follow when we look for the point of each paragraph. Then we can see the point of the whole passage or section. If you have trouble outlining 1:18-3:20, ask yourself what Paul is saying in each paragraph. (Some Bibles suggest paragraph divisions, while others leave it to you to decide where paragraphs would be.)

56

6. (*Optional*) Sketch an outline of 1:18-3:20 by giving titles to the main section and the subsections. The titles and subtitles in lessons one through five, as well as your own summaries of the passages, may help you.

1:18-3:20 _____

_____

1:18-32 _____

_____

2:1-16 _____

_____

2:17-29 _____

_____

3:1-8 _____

_____

3:9-20 _____

_____

For Further Study: If you haven't already done so, begin an outline of Romans with 1:1-3:20 on the blank pages at the end of this study guide.

For Thought and Discussion: Thinking about paragraphs may also help you follow 3:21-31. What is Paul's main point in 3:21-26? In 3:27-31? Now, what is the whole section about?

Justified through Christ (3:21-26)

Romans 1:18-3:20 was enough to make anyone worried. Righteousness never comes through lawkeeping because people just don't keep God's commands (3:20,23). Therefore, the wrath of God is being revealed. But now, having made his readers "conscious of sin" (3:20), Paul turns to the good news: "in the gospel a righteousness from God is revealed" (1:17). Read 3:21-31, noting in the margin any words or ideas you don't understand. Look them up in an English or Bible dictionary if the study guide doesn't explain them.

The Law and the Prophets (3:21). The whole Old Testament. Genesis 15:6, Psalm 32:1-2, and Habakkuk 2:4 all testify to this truth.

For Thought and Discussion: a. How does Paul emphasize that God's way of righteousness means declaring people righteous who fully deserve to be declared guilty (3:24-25)?

b. Why isn't justification a legal fiction (since we are declared not guilty even though we are guilty)? How is it fully just as well as generous to give us righteousness?

For Thought and Discussion: How does Jesus' death in our place prove God both just and merciful (3:26)?

Optional Application: Explain God's way of righteousness to someone.

Glory of God (3:23). "What God intended man to be. The glory that man had before the fall" (Genesis 1:26-28, Psalm 8:5-6, Ephesians 4:24).[2]

Justified (3:24). Declared righteous, not guilty. The guilty person's sins are declared to be paid in full, so he has a clear record before God.

Grace (3:24). See the note on 1:5,7 on page 28.

Redemption (3:24). Release by payment of a ransom. The image is of someone freeing a slave by buying him from his master, or someone paying a criminal's fine to release him from jail.

Sacrifice of atonement (3:25). "Propitiation" in KJV, NASB. "Expiation" in RSV. The penalty for sin (rebellion against God's will) is death (Romans 6:23), but God does not want sinners to die. The Old Testament sacrificial system was designed to illuminate both God's just hatred of sin and His merciful desire not to punish. God allowed men to kill animals in place of themselves. These sacrifices "atoned for" (covered) sin, "expiated" (removed) man's guilt, and "propitiated" (satisfied, appeased) God's justice. See Leviticus 16:11,15-16,20-22.

Romans 3:25b-26 explains that those Old Testament sacrifices were not sufficient payment for sin in themselves, but they were sufficient in that they represented what Christ was going to do. By putting faith in the sacrifices commanded to cleanse sin, the Israelites were putting faith in God's way of righteousness which is fully revealed in Christ. Thus, the sacrificial law testifies to God's way of righteousness by faith apart from works (3:21). Now, however, the sacrificial system is ended because the act it foreshadowed has occurred.

His blood (3:25). The sacrificial animal's shed blood signified the life that was being given up for the person's sin. Likewise, Christ's blood signifies the life He poured out for our sin and the death He accepted in our place.

Justification is a concept from the law courts. *Redemption* is from the slave market. *Atonement* is from the Temple.

7. In your own words, explain how Jesus has enabled us to become righteous if we put our faith in Him (3:24-25). (Consider: How does Jesus' death "redeem" us and "atone" for our sin?)

_____

_____

_____

_____

_____

_____

_____

8. Why is the phrase "freely by his grace" (3:24) important?

_____

_____

_____

_____

Implications (3:27-31)

9. Why does God's way of righteousness make it impossible for anyone to boast about himself (3:27-28)?

_____

_____

_____

_____

Optional Application: Do you feel more lovable and closer to God when you've been doing good things than when you've done wrong? Ask God to help you put your trust more actively in Jesus' death than in your own performance.

Optional Application: Meditate on God's justice and mercy. If you've had nagging feelings that God is demanding, unfair, vindictive, or soft on sin, confess those feelings and ask God to change your attitudes. (The book of Jonah is relevant here.)

Optional Application: Why is Christ's work important for you personally?

For Thought and Discussion: How does God's way of righteousness put both Jews and Gentiles on the same level before God (3:29-30)?

Optional Application: Are you ever tempted to feel superior to unbelievers or to Christians who live less righteously than you? If so, how does 3:27-30 affect your attitudes? Ask God to impress these truths within you.

For Further Study: On Romans 3:31, see Psalm 40:8, Jeremiah 31:33-34, Hebrews 9:14.

For Thought and Discussion: What does 1:18-3:20 reveal about God's character? What does 3:21-31 show about God and Christ?

10. How does righteousness by faith in Christ uphold God's Law (3:31)? See 3:9-20,23,25.

_____

_____

_____

_____

_____

Your response

11. What implications does 3:1-31 have for your life? Name as many as you can. (Consider the optional questions in the margins.)

_____

_____

_____

_____

_____

_____

12. Think about your answers to questions 3 and 11. What one implication of 3:1-31 would you like to concentrate on for application this week?

_____

_____

_____

_____

13. What action and prayer will you pursue in order to put this insight into practice?

_____

60

_____

_____

_____

_____

_____

For Further Study:
Add 3:1-31 to your
outline of Romans.

> **Study Skill—Application**
> You may find after awhile that application
> has become an effort to make yourself better,
> and that sheer effort is not making you more
> Christlike. When that happens, scale back
> your do-list, stop watching yourself for fail-
> ures, and take more time just thinking about
> Christ. Ask yourself if you are relying on God
> or self to enable you to suceed.

14. Reread 1:16-17. How would you summarize
    Paul's message in 1:18-3:31?

    _____

    _____

    _____

    _____

    _____

15. List any questions you have about 3:1-31.

    _____

    _____

    _____

    _____

For the group

You may want to take two weeks for this long lesson
or discuss just a few of the questions. The key concept is what God has done for us through Christ. Be

sure that everyone grasps the doctrines of atonement, justification, etc. But don't be satisfied until the group wrestles with how their actions and attitudes should be affected by these truths.

Warm-up. Here are two possibilities:

1. "Has your awareness of your own sin grown, lessened, or stayed the same since you became interested in following Christ? Can you explain why?"

2. "Do you feel that God likes to punish people who commit sins? What makes you feel that He does or doesn't?" The word *feel* here is deliberate; many people believe one thing about God in their heads but let their feelings about Him, acquired perhaps in traumatic childhood circumstances, govern their lives. Confronting our feelings can help us hear deep in our hearts the truth in 3:1-31 about God's character.

Read aloud.

Summarize.

Questions.

Evaluation. It is a good idea to evaluate your study after a few weeks so that you can improve it for the future. Here are two approaches to evaluation; you can select from both if you prefer:

1. Look at the goals you set at the beginning of this study. Are you doing the best you can to meet them? (For instance, in what ways are you getting to know God and each other better? Is the study encouraging you to grow more like Christ, or to know and act on the Bible better? If not, what is lacking, and how can you improve the study?)

2. Ask the group these three simple questions: What did you like best about this meeting? What did you like least? How could this study be changed to meet your needs better?

Worship. Praise God for His justice in judging sin and His mercy in providing a way to justify sinners. Thank Him for sacrificing Jesus for you. Praise His holy hatred of sin and His holy love for sinners.

The Law Court

To understand Paul's explanation of the gospel, we need to grasp the legal background. The Old Testament portrays God as a Sovereign who accepts the nation Israel as a subject people (a *vassal*). The agreement between Lord and vassal is called a *covenant* (treaty, pact, testament). This covenant legally binds the vassal to obey the Sovereign or face punishment. A person or the whole nation is "righteous" if he is in good standing with the Lord because he has kept the covenant. If he breaks the covenant, the Sovereign summons him into the royal court, tries him for treason, and sentences him (Deuteronomy 7:7-11, 29:9-15). All this is in accord with the legal systems of the ancient world.

At the same time, however, the Lord makes it clear that He is the King and Judge of not just Israel but the whole world (Genesis 18:25, Amos 1:3-2:16). Isaiah describes scenes in which the Lord summons the pagan nations into His throne room for trial and calls Israel as His witnesses (Isaiah 41:1,21-24,28-29; 43:8-13). In that trial, both Israel and the nations are declared unrighteous—guilty of treason and covenant-breaking. However, the Lord promises to reveal His own righteousness by forgiving and restoring the rebels.

How can He forgive the rebels without breaking His own law that requires traitors to die? Isaiah 52:13-53:12 finds the solution in the laws of sacrifice for atonement. The Lord will raise up a Servant who will die as "a guilt offering" (Leviticus 5:16, 6:5; Isaiah 53:10) for the people. That substitute death will satisfy the law of capital punishment for treason. Isaiah stresses that this Servant will be guiltless Himself (Isaiah 53:9), for the law requires an unblemished offering for any sacrifice (Leviticus 1:3-4, Malachi 1:8).

1. *The NIV Study Bible,* page 1709.
2. *The NIV Study Bible,* page 1710.

ROMANS 4:1-25

Abraham's Righteousness

No one may boast of his favor with God, for both Jew and Gentile are declared righteous not because of obedience to God's Law but because of faith in Jesus' death (3:27). This was a hard idea for Jews to grasp. What about Abraham, the father of the nation, whom the Jews considered the most obedient man there ever was? Surely he had reason to boast of God's approval! Paul knew if he could prove that Abraham had no reason to boast, then the matter was settled for any Jew.

Read 4:1-25 for its overall message. Ask God to show you what it means to be accepted totally by grace, regardless of your works.

Works or faith? (4:1-8)

Abraham believed God (4:3). See the box, "Abraham's Faith" on page 72.

Credited (4:3,4,5,6,9,10,11,22,23,24) and *count* (4:8). "Counted," "reckoned," and "imputed" in KJV. This word from the marketplace means "to put to someone's account." Both gifts and wages are credited to a person's account (4:4).

But not before God (4:2). Or, "But this is not how God sees him."[1] That is, *if* Abraham was justified by works, *then* he could boast, but in God's eyes Abraham was not justified by works.

For Thought and Discussion: Are you ever tempted to think of faith as a virtue that earns God's favor? Why is this wrong?

For Thought and Discussion: a. How does a wicked person become guiltless before God (4:5)?
b. What implications does this have for our lives?

65

For Thought and Discussion: Why does trusting God to justify the ungodly glorify Him more than trying to earn His acceptance?

For Thought and Discussion:
a. Does trusting God to justify us allow us to persist in willful sin? Why or why not? (Paul discusses this in chapter 6.)

b. Have you ever excused a sin by telling yourself that God would forgive you? If so, how can you avoid doing this again?

Optional Application: Meditate on God's character in 4:5 and your status in 4:7-8. Examine your life for ways in which you are still acting as though you have to earn God's love. Thank Him for His generous forgiveness.

1. Why was Abraham's faith not a work that earned the wage of righteousness? (Consider: According to Romans 4:4-5, what was Abraham believing about God?)

_____

_____

_____

_____

_____

2. In Psalm 32:1-2, David describes what God does when He credits righteousness to a person. How does David describe what God does (Romans 4:6-8)?

_____

_____

_____

_____

Circumcision or uncircumcision?
(4:9-12)

Not after, but before (Romans 4:10). God pronounced Abraham righteous (Genesis 15:6) some fourteen years before he was circumcised (Genesis 17:23-24).

3. Remember the Jews' beliefs about circumcision (page 48). Why was it important that God declared Abraham righteous before he was circumcised (Romans 4:9-11)?

_____

_____

_____

For Further Study:
a. How does James 2:14-26 (especially 2:24) complement Romans 4:1-8?
b. For the same balance, compare Ephesians 2:8-9 to Ephesians 2:10, or Genesis 15:6 to Genesis 22.

4. Circumcision was a sign (pointer) and seal (outward ratification and guarantee) of the righteousness Abraham had by faith (4:11). What are the signs and seals of a Christian's righteousness by faith? (*Optional:* See John 13:35; Acts 2:41, 8:12, 10:47; Ephesians 1:13-14, 4:30; 1 Peter 3:21.)

_____

_____

_____

_____

5. Abraham is the physical forefather of all who are physically Jews (4:1). Of whom is he the spiritual forefather?

4:11 _____

_____

4:12 _____

_____

Law or faith? (4:13-16)

Through law (4:13). On the basis of fully obeying God's Law in the future.

Live by law (4:14). Base their claim to inheritance on fully obeying the Law.

6. a. On what basis did Abraham receive the promise of inheriting the world? What requirements, if any, would he and his descendants have to fulfill (4:13)?

67

For Further Study:
How does law bring
wrath (4:15)? Paul
explains in 7:7-11.

**For Thought and
Discussion:** Does it
seem fair that even
sinners can inherit
God's promises if they
put faith in God? Why
or why not?

**For Thought and
Discussion:** How are
justification by faith
and justification by
grace related
(3:24-25, 4:16)?

b. How does this apply to you this week?

_____

_____

_____

_____

_____

7. God's promise is worthless if the only people
who can inherit it are those who live up to it by
perfect obedience (4:14-15). Why would this
requirement make the promise worthless?

_____

_____

_____

_____

_____

Sight or faith? (4:17-25)

Who gives life to the dead (4:17). Abraham believed
that God could bring life from Sarah's dead
womb (Romans 4:19) and that if he sacrificed
his son Isaac in obedience to God, then God
would raise Isaac from the dead to fulfill His
promise of descendants through Isaac (Genesis
22).

Calls things that are not (Romans 4:17). Abraham
knew that God created the world from nothing
and could create a son and a myriad of nations
from what looked like nothing.

8. What facts might have convinced Abraham that God's promise of a son was impossible (4:19)?

_____

_____

_____

_____

9. However, Abraham believed two things about God that convinced him that God could keep His promise (4:17).

   a. In what ways does God give "life to the dead" (4:17)? (*Optional:* See Romans 4:24-25, 8:13; Luke 9:23-24; 1 Corinthians 15:20-22; 2 Corinthians 4:11-12,16-18; Ephesians 2:4-5.)

   _____

   _____

   _____

   _____

   _____

   b. How does God call "things that are not as though they were" (4:17)? (*Optional:* See Romans 8:18-25; 1 Corinthians 1:18-31; 2 Corinthians 5:1,6-10; Hebrews 10:35-11:2; 1 John 3:2-3.)

   _____

   _____

   _____

   _____

For Thought and Discussion: How was Abraham able to resist the temptation to doubt God's promise (4:20)? What lesson does this offer us?

Optional Application: How can you give "glory to God" in your current circumstances as Abraham did (4:20)?

Optional Application: Does Romans 4:17 motivate you to trust God to do anything specific in your life? If so, what are you trusting Him to do? Tell Him about your hopes.

Delivered . . . sins . . . raised . . . justification (4:25). "For" here means "on account of." Jesus was delivered to death in order to atone for our sins, and He was raised to guarantee our justification and encourage us to put faith in that jus-

Optional Application: Meditate on 4:25 and its significance for you. Thank God for delivering over and raising Jesus.

tification. Of course, Paul doesn't mean that Christ's death had nothing to do with justification, nor that His resurrection had nothing to do with atonement.[2]

Your response

10. How has Abraham's example in 4:1-25 helped you to understand righteousness by grace through faith? Summarize what Paul says in this chapter.

_____

_____

_____

_____

_____

11. What insight from 4:1-25 seems most relevant to you?

_____

_____

_____

_____

12. How can you put this insight into practice or let it affect your life this week?

_____

_____

_____

_____

_____

13. List any questions you have about 4:1-25.

_____

_____

_____

_____

For Further Study:
Add chapter 4 to your
outline.

For the group

Accountability. At your last few meetings, you have
each named certain areas of your lives on which you
wanted to concentrate for growth. You planned to
pray for each other, think about Paul's words during
the week, look for chances to act obediently, consistently confess and seek forgiveness, and so on. At
the beginning of this meeting, you might each
report briefly on how well you followed through on
your commitments, and what happened.

For example, one person may have gotten
stuck scheduling time to pray, another may have
had trouble remembering Paul's words during the
day, and another may have noticed for the first time
how self-righteous he really is. This reporting back
will update you on how to pray for each other and
will let you share ideas for how to schedule prayer,
remember God's Word during the day, and so on.

Warm-up. Ask, "What chance have you had this
week to act on faith in one of God's promises?"
Even if most group members can't think of answers
right away, this question will start them thinking
about how 4:1-25 applies to them.

Questions. Use the subtitles in this lesson to shape
your discussion. They should help the group trace
Paul's train of thought. For example:

According to 4:1-8, how do we know that Abraham was justified by faith, not works?
Why is it important that Abraham was declared
righteous before being circumcised
(4:9-12)?
Why is faith a better basis for God's promises
than law (4:13-16)?
How did Abraham live by faith rather than
sight (4:17-25)?

71

At each stage, discuss how you can follow Abraham's example. Verses 17-25, in particular, are a challenge to act in faith. Encourage group members to share how they plan to apply Abraham's example.

Restating. In even the best study guide, a question is occasionally unclear. Also, groups often find it helpful and more interesting when leaders rephrase the questions instead of just repeating them. So, when you want to restate a question, keep these two sets of categories in mind: 1) the procedure of observe-interpret-apply; and 2) the topics of "Who is God?" "Who am I?" and "What should I do?"

For example, you can restate an observation question like this: "What does this verse (or paragraph) say about God or Christ (His character, acts, etc.)?" Or, "What does this verse (or paragraph) say about man's unredeemed nature or his nature/identity in Christ?" Or, "What does this paragraph say we should think or do because we are in Christ?"

For interpretation questions, you can ask, "What does the phrase: '. . .' mean?" Or, "What is Paul trying to tell us about God (or Christ, or man, or what we should do)?"

For applications, try asking, "How does this passage apply to you?" Or, "What implications does this passage have for your life?" Or, "What specific steps can you take to act on this teaching?"

Worship. Thank God for the example of Abraham's faith. Thank Him for not demanding faith as a work, but only as simple trust. Thank Him for His promises. Praise Him for being "the God who gives life to the dead and calls things that are not as though they were."

Abraham's Faith

The Jews of Paul's day held that Abraham was justified by his deeds, his sinlessness, and they used Genesis 15:6 as the supreme proof of this fact. According to Rabbi Shemaiah (about 50 BC), God had said, "The faith with which their father Abraham believed in me merits that I should divide the sea for them, as it is written: 'And he believed in the LORD, and he counted it to him

(continued on page 73)

72

(continued from page 72)
for righteousness.'"[3] The same work later said, "Our father Abraham became the heir of this and of the coming world simply by the merit of the faith with which he believed in the LORD, as it is written: 'He believed in the LORD. . . .'"[4]

In short, the Jews regarded Abraham's faith as the greatest of his many meritorious works. By contrast, Paul insisted that 1) Abraham was not sinless, and 2) Abraham's faith did not earn righteousness but moved God to gift him with righteousness.

God promised that Abraham would have a son and a multitude of descendants from his own body (Genesis 15:1-5), and Abraham believed Him (Genesis 15:6). That trust in God's willingness and ability to keep His promises moved God to treat Abraham as a loyal subject, even though Abraham fell far short of sinlessness. Abraham did many acts of obedience that reflected his faith; for instance, he proceeded to sacrifice his son until God allowed him to stop (Genesis 22). However, Abraham also did many acts of faithlessness that God forgave; for example, he twice lied about his wife and risked losing her (Genesis 12:10-20, 20:1-18). Those occasional lapses did not forfeit Abraham's righteousness because perfect performance had not earned that righteousness.

1. Crandall, page 84.
2. Murray, pages 154-157; Bruce, *Romans,* page 119; Cranfield, page 97.
3. *Mekilta* on Exodus 14:15, quoted in Cranfield, pages 84-85.
4. *Mekilta* on Exodus 14:31, quoted in Cranfield, page 85.

ROMANS 5:1-21

Fruits of Righteousness

We now reach a bridge chapter in Paul's letter. Some commentators group chapter 5 with 1:18-4:25 because it summarizes justification and its effects. Other people group chapter 5 with 6:1-8:39 because it begins to describe the life that justified people live by faith. So, as you read 5:1-21, decide how you think it relates to what has gone before. You might compare the outlines on page 24 to one in a handbook or study Bible.

1. Briefly summarize Paul's reasoning in 1:18-4:25.

   _____

   _____

   _____

   _____

   _____

   _____

Peace with God (5:1-11)

Peace (5:1), *access* (5:2), *enemies . . . reconciled* (5:10). Paul envisions God as a King whose subjects rebelled. While war raged, those enemy

75

For Further Study:
Define reconciliation, using an English dictionary.

For Thought and Discussion: How is "peace with God" different from peace of mind?

For Thought and Discussion: What is the "grace in which we now stand" (5:2)?

For Thought and Discussion: Why are reconciliation and peace as important as justification?

subjects were unable to approach their Lord. However, the Sovereign has sent His Son to achieve reconciliation between the rebels and the King, so now the reconciled subjects have access to the throne room.

2. How were you formerly God's enemy (5:10), at war with Him?

_____

_____

_____

_____

_____

Study Skill—Parallelism
Parallel structure can often be a clue to Paul's meaning, but we must draw our conclusions carefully. Parallel does not mean identical in meaning. Notice the parallelism in 5:9-10:

5:9	5:10
justified	reconciled
by his blood	through the death of his Son
how much more	how much more
shall we be saved	shall we be saved
from God's wrath through him?	through his life[1]

---

3. Romans 5:1-11 tells what is true of our lives because we have been justified and reconciled to God. List as many benefits of justification and peace as you can find in 5:1-11.

_____

_____

_____

_____

_____

_____

_____

Hope (5:2,4-5). Not a mood of wishfulness, but rather something that we expect with certainty. We have a sure expectation of attaining "the glory of God" (5:2) and salvation from God's wrath at the Judgment (5:9-10).

Glory of God (5:2). See the note on 3:23, page 58. See also 2 Corinthians 3:18, Philippians 3:21, 1 John 3:2-3, Romans 8:18-30.

_____

4. One benefit of our peace is "the hope of the glory of God" (5:2).

   a. What is the connection between suffering and hope (5:3-4)?

_____

_____

_____

_____

   b. Why does hope not disappoint us (5:5)?

_____

_____

_____

_____

   c. How could the hope of the glory of God affect your attitude toward your current circumstances or aims in life?

_____

_____

_____

For Thought and Discussion: a. Does suffering always produce endurance? Why or why not?

   b. How does faith enable a person to let his suffering produce endurance and hope rather than bitterness and despair? How is this fact relevant to you?

For Thought and Discussion: Why does Jesus' death for us as sinners and enemies assure us that we will be saved from God's wrath at the Judgment (5:6-10)?

Optional Application: Are you ever tempted to doubt God's love for you or your safety from judgment? If so, meditate on the security that Jesus' death gives us (5:6-10).

Optional Application: Meditate daily on your hope of glory or the good results of suffering (5:2-5). Remind yourself of this each time you are tempted to grumble or despair about your circumstances.

For Thought and Discussion: What hinders you from letting hope fill you with joy in the midst of your circumstances? Or, what keeps you from taking full advantage of your access to God? Pray about this.

For Thought and Discussion: How does 5:1-11 show the Trinity working in harmony? What does each Person do?

_____

_____

_____

5. God's love firmly proves the security of our hope, says Paul (5:5). How has God demonstrated His love for us (5:6-8)?

_____

_____

_____

_____

6. Paul says we should respond to peace with God and hope of glory with joy and exultation (5:2-3,11). What sorts of things can keep you from responding like this?

_____

_____

_____

7. How can you make sure you stay focused on your reasons for joy this week?

_____

_____

_____

_____

_____

Study Skill—Application

Here are some of the most frequent obstacles to applying God's Word:

1. "I didn't have time to meditate on and

(continued on page 79)

78

(continued from page 78)
pray about a passage this week." Answer: What do you think about while in the car, getting dressed, or doing other things besides working and talking? Most people have at least a few minutes a day in which they can think about God rather than earthly concerns. Try turning off the radio and television, and just being quiet or noisy with God.

2. "I forget to think about Scripture during my free moments." Make reminders: tape a card with a reminder or quotation to your dashboard, refrigerator, desk, or mirror. Tie a string on your finger, purse, or briefcase. Try any gimmick that helps! It's important to let the Scripture come to mind frequently during the day.

3. "I can't ever think of specific ways to act on what the Scripture says." Divide your life into spheres (home, work, church, school . . .) or people (spouse, children, co-workers, boss, church friends . . .). Choose one person, and pray about what that person needs from you, what might prevent you from fulfilling that need, and how you might fulfill that need. Or, review a recent situation in which you sinned. Look for a similar situation in the near future to act rightly. Ask God to enable you to recognize and respond rightly to the situation.

Persistent prayer, inviting God to show you opportunities to apply what you have learned, will be answered.

From Adam to Christ (5:12-21)

On the one hand, 5:12-21 sums up Paul's explanation of justification by grace. On the other hand, this passage lays the groundwork for us to understand chapter 6, living in light of our union with Christ. The key concept in 5:12-21 is hard for modern people to grasp because it is alien to our individualistic way of thinking. This key is that:

1. Adam was a real historical person, just like Jesus.

2. The human race is a unity, a federation, like

79

For Thought and Discussion: a. In what sense do people who do not know God's Law (such as the people who lived between Adam and Moses, and people in many countries today) sin? See 1:18-21,28; 2:12,14-15.

b. In what sense are those people not able to sin (5:13-14)?

c. Why do those people die anyway (5:12-14)?

the cells in a body. Adam was the head of the race. Therefore, his decision to sin affects us as surely as a person's decisions in his head affect the rest of his body. Or, to change the image, Adam's decision to declare war on God put all his descendants at war, just as a prince's declaration affects his citizens. This might not seem fair, but:

a. we simply are affected by Adam's decision;
b. each one of us repeats Adam's rebellion in our own acts;
c. our connectedness as a race is also what allows Christ's death to affect us.

With this concept of human solidarity in mind, read 5:12-21. Look for the comparison and contrast between Adam and Christ.

Adam's effect (5:12-14)

8. What two things did Adam introduce into the world and pass on to his descendants (5:12)?

_____

Because all sinned (5:12). Two interpretations of this phrase are possible:

1. *Each person dies because he personally sins.*[2] The chief merit of this interpretation is that it follows the most obvious meaning of "all sinned." Had Paul meant something else, would he not have said something else? Also, Paul says God will judge each person according to his own deeds (2:6,12) and that everyone sins (1:18-32).

2. *Each person dies because he is part of the human race, all of which sinned when its representative head (Adam) sinned.*[3] In reply to the objection that Paul did not say "all sinned in Adam," interpreters say that Paul implies this in 5:12,15,17-19. Unborn babies do not die because of their own sins, and Paul says that people who don't know the Law die without ever breaking an explicit command of God (5:13-14).

Christians who hold either (1) or (2) agree that Adam's descendants all inherit his sinful nature, his will to sin. Those who die before they get a chance to commit a sinful act are just as corrupt by nature as those who live long enough to act out their sinfulness. We are not sinful because we sin; we sin because we are sinful. (See Genesis 6:5, 8:21; Psalm 51:5, 58:3.) It is our solidarity with Adam that makes us all die and all sin.

Sin by breaking a command, as did Adam (5:14). "Adam's transgression" in KJV. "The offense of Adam" in NASB. The Greek word for "transgression" means breaking a known law.

Jesus more than Adam (5:15-19)

Pattern (5:14). A "type" (Greek: *typos*) is literally a mold or pattern. In the Bible, it is a person or thing in the Old Testament that prefigures a person or thing of the Messianic Age.[4] The resemblance between the Old Testament type and the New Testament "antitype" is limited and should not be pushed too far. For this reason, Paul takes care to show how Adam and Jesus are different (5:15-17) before he explains how they are alike (5:18-19).

9. In 5:15-17, Paul contrasts Adam and Jesus. In the chart below, list the effects of Adam's trespass and God's gift (Jesus) named in 5:15-17.

Adam	Jesus

For Thought and Discussion: When Paul says "the many" in 5:18-19, does he mean that every person will be justified and saved? What condition does he state in 5:17?

For Thought and Discussion: How did Jesus make us righteous before God (5:18-19)?

10. Paul repeats "how much more" and "one . . . many" to show the difference between Adam and Jesus. Why is Jesus' effect "much more" than Adam's (5:15-17)?

_____

_____

_____

_____

_____

11. Paul also repeats the words "gift" and "grace" in 5:15-17,20-21. How are these words important to the difference between Adam and Jesus?

_____

_____

_____

_____

_____

_____

Jesus like Adam (5:18-19)

12. Now that the contrast between Adam and Christ is clear, Paul can finish explaining the resemblance that he began to explain in 5:12. Using the phrase, "just as . . . so also" in 5:18 and 5:19, show the resemblance between Adam's and Jesus' deeds in the chart below.

Adam	Jesus
just as . . .	*so also . . .*

82

Adam	Jesus

For Thought and Discussion: In what way does grace increase when sin increases (5:20)?

The Law's effect (5:20-21)

13. Men were sinners (rebels) by nature before they knew God's Law, for they inherited Adam's enemy status and sinful nature (5:10,12,19). However, what effect did God's righteous Law have on rebellious people (5:20; compare 7:13)?

_____

_____

_____

_____

_____

14. Why did God want His Law to have this effect (5:20-21)?

_____

_____

_____

_____

_____

_____

15. Observe the repeated word "reign" in 5:17,21. What reigns for people who choose solidarity with . . .

Adam? _____

Jesus? _____

83

For Further Study:
Add 5:1-21 to your
outline if you think
3:21-5:21 is a unit. If
you think chapter 5
belongs with chapters
6-8, you can wait and
outline it all at once.

**Optional
Application:** a. How
can you act out the
truth of reigning in
life this week?

b. Who can you
tell what you have
learned about Adam
and Christ?

c. How can hav-
ing the status of
being righteous rather
than sinful before God
affect your life right
now? (Recall
5:1-5,11.)

16. Summarize 5:12-21.

_____

_____

_____

_____

_____

Your response

17. You may have planned an application already in
question 7. If not, what one insight from 5:1-21
would you like to concentrate on this week?

_____

_____

_____

_____

18. How can you let it affect your thoughts and
actions?

_____

_____

_____

_____

_____

19. List your questions about 5:1-21.

_____

_____

_____

_____

For the group

Warm-up. To help the group understand more about human solidarity, ask members to name some ways in which they have benefitted undeservingly from being born in this century, this country, and their particular families. For example, you have electric lights and penicillin not because you have each invented them, but because fellow humans invented them and passed them on to you. You have healthy (or sick) bodies partly because your ancestors gave you certain traits, your parents fed you a certain way, and your contemporaries surround you with a certain environment and means of health care. You get all these things, for good or ill, just by being born.

Note: Many political and religious groups use "human solidarity," or "the brotherhood of man," to promote their views and agendas. Human solidarity is a fact, but we must carefully examine the implications people draw from this fact. Some of those supposed implications are illogical, false, and inconsistent with other parts of Scripture.

Peace with God. This section deals with 5:1,9-10 before 5:2-8 because verses 1 and 9-10 are about the same thing: peace or reconciliation. Paul mentions it at the beginning and end to frame the passage, and verses 9-10 help to explain what Paul means by peace.

When you talk about peace, hope, love, and joy, first define what each of these is. Use the word definitions in this guide, cross-references, a dictionary, and the context of 1:18-5:11.

Joy is partly something we decide to have, and partly something that grows out of meditating on the peace, hope, and love we have because of our reconciliation. However, we can remind ourselves to be joyful when circumstances tempt us not to be. Encourage the group to keep joy and the reasons for it in mind this week.

Adam and Christ. To organize this section, draw two charts on marker board or large paper. Let the group fill in one to show how Jesus is like (or opposite to) Adam (question 12), and the other to show how Jesus is "much more" than Adam (questions 9 and 10).

Why is this comparison important for our lives? How should it affect the way you think and act?

Worship. Thank God for the reconciliation, love, and hope He has given you. If you sing together, choose songs with these themes to reinforce them. Also, praise God for making our race interconnected, so that Jesus' one death can affect all of us. Thank Him for revealing His plan to you personally.

Wrap-up. Next week, plan to share how meditating on your peace and hope has affected your outlook.

1. *The NIV Study Bible,* page 1712.
2. Cranfield, pages 113-114.
3. Bruce, *Romans,* page 129; Murray, pages 182-187; Hodge, pages 148-155.
4. Cranfield, page 117.

ROMANS 6:1-14

United with Christ

Paul has shown that all of us are guilty before God. All of us—even Abraham—are acquitted of guilt and reconciled with God only by the gracious gift of Jesus. We were united with Adam in his sin and death, but we can choose to become united with Christ in His righteousness and life.

This free gift of grace, received only by faith, unearned by any obedience to God's Law, raises a serious problem for many people. Can we ignore God's commands, do what we please, and claim righteousness before God based merely on faith in Jesus' death? Paul has asserted that "where sin increased, grace increased all the more" (5:20). No wonder Paul's opponents claimed he said, "'Let us do evil that good may result'" (3:8)! If sin doesn't subject you again to God's judgment, and if sin positively enhances His glory and increases His grace, then why not sin?

In 3:8, Paul merely condemned this notion without comment, but in chapter 6 he refutes it. Anyone who entertains this idea does not understand what Paul has said about sin and righteousness, about union with Adam and with Christ.

Read 6:1-14, noting especially the words "death," "life," "united with," "sin," and "righteousness."

1. Chapter 6 answers the question, "Why should a justified person not sin?" What is the basic reason why we should abandon sin (6:2)?

_____

_____

_____

_____

How we died (6:3-10)

In 6:3-10, Paul explains how we died to sin.

Baptized into his death (6:3). Christ's death is effective atonement for a person when he puts faith in Christ, even before he is baptized. But baptism is 1) God's public proclamation that He is accepting Christ's death as satisfaction for this particular believer's sins, and 2) the believer's public proclamation that he is accepting Christ as satisfaction for his sins and Lord of his life.[1]

Buried (6:4). Burial is a public acknowledgment, ratification, and seal that the person in question has died. Like burial, baptism is not the death of the old self but the rite which publicly confirms that a death has occurred.[2]

2. a. When Christ was crucified, why was death given mastery or dominion over Him (2 Corinthians 5:21; Isaiah 53:4-6,11-12; Romans 4:25; 5:21)?

_____

_____

_____

_____

b. However, after Christ died and was raised, why did neither sin nor death any longer have mastery over Him (6:7,9-10)?

_____

88

_____

_____

_____

_____

Old self (6:6). Literally, "old man." "The *whole* of our fallen human nature, the whole self in its fallenness."[3] No part of a person escapes condemnation and death in God's sight when the person unites with Christ. In this way, a wholly new self can be born, a completely "new creation" (2 Corinthians 5:17, Galatians 2:20).

Body of sin (6:6). The old, unregenerate self, dominated by sin. It includes the physical, emotional, psychological, intellectual, and spiritual self.[4]

3. a. Why did death have mastery over us (5:12,17; 6:23)?

_____

_____

_____

_____

b. What happened to us when we were "baptized into his [Christ's] death" (6:3)? Explain Paul's following statements in your own words.

we were "buried with" Christ (6:4)

_____

_____

_____

_____

89

we were "united with him in his death"
(NASB: "in the likeness of His death," 6:5)

_____

_____

_____

_____

"our old self was crucified with him so that
the body of sin might be done away with"
(6:6, NIV 1984)

_____

_____

_____

_____

_____

we were made "no longer . . . slaves to sin"
(6:6) and were "freed from sin" (6:7)

_____

_____

_____

_____

Study Skill—Paraphrasing
Restating a verse in your own words, as you
did in question 3, is often a good way to see
if you understand it. When in doubt, ask a
mature Christian whether your paraphrase is
accurate, or how it could be improved.

How we live (6:11-14)

4. Our death is a single, finished work, signified by
   the rite of baptism, our burial. How does Paul
   describe the ongoing moral effects of our death?

6:4 _____

_____

6:5 _____

_____

6:8,10 _____

_____

For Thought and Discussion: What does it mean to "live a new life" (6:4)?

5. Christ has "died to sin" and "lives to God" (6:10), and so does the believer who identifies with Christ (6:8). What does it mean to live to God?

_____

_____

_____

_____

_____

6. What, then, should a believer do?

6:11 _____

_____

_____

6:12-13a _____

_____

_____

6:13b _____

_____

_____

7. Why is it necessary to "count" or "reckon" (KJV) ourselves dead to sin and alive to God (6:11)?

_____

_____

91

Optional Application: a. How can you actively reject the reign of sin in your life this week?
    b. How can you offer the parts of your body to righteousness?

Optional Application: Meditate on the fact of your death and new life. Look for ways to act on this fact.

For Thought and Discussion: In what sense is sin no longer our "master" (6:14) even though we do still succumb to it sometimes? See 6:15-8:17.

For Thought and Discussion: What does 6:1-14 tell us about God and Christ?

For Further Study: Outline 6:1-14, and add it to the rest of your outline. Or wait until after lesson ten.

8. Pray about 6:11-13. What are some practical ways in which you can fulfill these commands this week?

_____

_____

_____

_____

_____

Not under law (6:14). Christians are freed from the condemnation and penalties God's Law required. Instead, they are judged according to the gracious intervention of Jesus. Also, apart from grace, people can only try to meet God's expectations by their own effort, but grace empowers believers to live up to what God desires. Paul expands on 6:14 in chapters 7-8.

9. Summarize Paul's point in 6:1-14.

_____

_____

_____

_____

10. List any questions you have about 6:1-14.

_____

_____

92

For the group

Application. Take five or ten minutes to discuss how your efforts to apply Romans are going. (Have you been able to follow through on your plans for meditation, prayer, and action? If not, what gets in the way? Has meditating on the truths about God affected your actions or outlook in any ways?)

Some people get discouraged if they don't see permanent changes in themselves after struggling with an application for a week. Tell such people not to worry if they aren't seeing big results, as long as they are being diligent in prayer, meditation, and the search for ways to apply. Other people don't feel interested in devoting energy to application over an extended period. Urge them to see their desperate need to work at this. You might want to discuss the Study Skills on pages 61 and 78-79.

Warm-up. Both 5:12-21 and 6:1-14 have to do with being united with Christ. Ask each person to think of one time in the past week when he or she did something expressly because he or she is united with Christ. Tell group members that if they can't think of something they *did* do, then they should think of something they *could have* done. For instance, "because I am 'in Christ' rather than 'in Adam,' I choose to forgive George for letting me down yesterday."

You can return to this question when you discuss 6:11-13 (questions 6-8). How could group members have *reckoned* themselves dead to sin and *offered* their bodies to God? Thinking about past opportunities can help you notice future ones when they arrive.

Outlining the passage after your personal study can help you organize your thoughts to lead the group study. The subheads in the study guide suggest a possible outline. Be sure to have a grip on the logic and main point of a passage before you lead a discussion. If you're confused, is there any hope for the group?

Questions. Questions 2 and 3 are related: death had dominion over Christ because He identified with us; it has no more dominion over us because we identify with Him.

Baptism is a point of contention for some people. At one extreme, some hold that it is necessary for salvation; at the other, some feel it is unimportant and may be disregarded. Explore this issue if your group sees a need to do so. Consult trustworthy books if necessary. Your pastor may be able to suggest some.

This study instead stresses the meaning of baptism for the believer, and personal applications for you. Discuss some possible ways in which it is relevant for each of you.

Worship. Praise God for burying you with Christ, putting your old self to death, raising you to life with Christ, and putting you under grace rather than law. Ask Him to help you count yourself dead to sin and alive to Him.

1. Cranfield, pages 130-131; *The NIV Study Bible*, page 1713; Bruce, page 136; Murray, page 214.
2. Bruce, page 138; Cranfield, page 132.
3. Cranfield, page 134.
4. Charles Hodge, *Commentary of the Epistle to the Romans* (Eerdmans, 1947 [1864]), page 197; Cranfield, page 134; Bruce, pages 138-139; *The NIV Study Bible*, page 1714. But compare Murray, pages 220-221.

ROMANS 6:15-7:6

Under Grace

Why not sin? One reason is our unity with Christ
that makes us alive to God (6:1-14). God and grace,
not sin and death, are our master (5:17,21; 6:9,14).
But this suggests another objection. If death (the
Law's punishment for sin) has no more power over
us, then fear of the Law cannot restrain us from fla-
grant wickedness. Does our freedom from sin, death,
and the Law's penalties mean that we can ignore all
moral standards (6:14-15)?

To answer this objection, Paul explains what it
means to live "under grace." He begins with the
metaphor of master and slave from 6:14, then uses
an illustration from marriage. Read 6:14-7:6, looking for Paul's answer to the question, "What does it
mean to be 'not under law, but under grace'?"

Slavery (6:15-23)

1. List all the ways Paul describes being "under
grace" in 6:15-23. (See 6:16,18,22.)

_____

_____

_____

_____

_____

95

For Thought and Discussion: Why does Paul speak of slavery to "obedience" in 6:16, "righteousness" in 6:18-19, and "God" in 6:22? How are these ideas related?

For Thought and Discussion: What evidence can you offer to support or refute Paul's claim in 6:21 that sin has no benefits which outweigh its costs? (*Optional:* See Ecclesiastes 5:10,15-17; 11:9-12:8.)

Form of teaching (6:17). This is probably the basic doctrines of the gospel and its implications for life which new converts received. This teaching probably included ethical instruction, such as Matthew 5:1-7:27 and Colossians 3:1-4:6.

2. With what attitude do believers obey their new master (6:17)?

_____

_____

_____

3. Think about yourself and the people you know. What benefits do people often *think* they reap from self-serving deeds?

_____

_____

_____

_____

_____

4. However, what "wage" does a person enslaved to sin earn (6:16,21,23)?

_____

_____

_____

5. Why is it impossible to be our own master— enslaved neither to sin nor to God?

_____

_____

_____

96

_____

_____

_____

6. a. The results of choosing to be a slave to obedience are a progression. Trace that
progression.

Obedience leads to _____

_____ (6:16), which leads to

_____ (6:19), which leads to

_____ (6:22).

b. Why are these results "the gift of God" (6:23)
rather than a wage earned for obedience
(4:4-5)? See 3:23-24; 5:19; 6:6-7,18.

_____

_____

_____

_____

_____

_____

_____

_____

Human terms (6:19). Paul explains why he uses the
imperfect, human analogy of slavery to describe
our relationship to God. In some ways it is
wholly inappropriate, but in other ways it
expresses important truths.

7. a. In what ways is our relationship to God like
slavery?

_____

_____

_____

97

For Thought and Discussion: Why are many people afraid to release themselves, their teenage children, or other people from rules and penalties? Why is it essential that they do release them?

Optional Application: Specifically how can you show your whole-hearted obedience to God rather than to sin this week? If you need ideas, skim Romans 12-13.

b. In what ways is our relationship to God not like slavery (John 15:15; Romans 6:17,22-23)?

_____

_____

_____

_____

_____

8. To summarize 6:15-23, explain: Why will a person freed from the Law's penalties choose not to disobey God?

_____

_____

_____

_____

_____

The marriage analogy (7:1-6)

Paul has shown why people who are truly living under grace will labor not to sin (6:15-23). But in case some readers aren't convinced that Christians are freed from the law as well as from sin (6:14), Paul uses the analogy of marriage to explain.

Men who know the law (7:1). Both Jewish and Roman law embraced the legal principle Paul states in 7:1.[1]

98

Married woman (7:2). Romans 7:2-3 is not an exact allegory of 7:4, as though the wife=us and the husband=the Law. Rather, 7:2-3 illustrates Paul's point in 7:1. Notice that in 7:4 the Law hasn't died; it still lives to require death for sinners, either by identification with Christ or by eternal punishment. Instead, *we* have died in Christ, so we are freed from further penalty.

---

9. A woman is free from the law of adultery if her husband dies because the law has authority only over living people (7:1-3). Therefore, why are we free from the Law that condemns transgressors to death (7:4)?

_____

_____

_____

_____

_____

10. Now that we are no longer bound to sin by the Law, we belong to a new husband. To whom do we now belong (7:4)?

_____

11. Also, now that we are freed from the Law's condemnation, what are we free to do?

"in order that . . ." (7:4) _____

_____

_____

"so that . . ." (7:6) _____

_____

_____

12. Did the Law ever enable us to do these things? What did it do to us (7:5)?

_____

For Thought and Discussion: How has Paul shown why we are neither legalists obeying mere rules nor libertines obeying no rules?

For Further Study: When Paul says we died to the Law (7:4), does he mean that we were released only from its condemnation or also from its moral guidance? Should a Christian freed from the Law still try to obey the Ten Commandments? (See Romans 3:31; 7:12,14a,25; 8:4; 13:8-10; Matthew 5:17-48.)

For Thought and Discussion: Why does Paul contrast "Spirit" with "written code" (literally, "letter") in 7:6, rather than "Spirit" with "Law"? See 7:14a.

Optional Application: Ask God to show you how to obey according to the Spirit rather than the written code (7:6). Ask Him to enable you to obey joyfully rather than out of fear of failure. Look for one specific act of obedience you could do this week.

Optional Application: What difference does it make to your life that you have died to the Law, so that its penalties no longer bind you? How does this fact affect your attitudes toward your own and others' responsibilities? Meditate this week on your freedom from penalties (7:4,6), thank God for this fact daily, and remind yourself of it each time you are tempted to do good to win approval.

For Thought and Discussion: What did you learn about God and Christ from 6:15-7:6?

In newness of the Spirit (7:6, NASB). Paul explains this way of service in chapter 8. He explains 7:5 in 7:7-13.

13. Reread 6:15-7:6. What one truth from this passage do you most want to remember and apply?

14. How can you begin to let this truth affect your habits this week? Write down at least one concrete step you can take.

15. List any questions you have about 6:15-7:6.

For the group

Warm-up. Question 3 may be a good warm-up. Ask group members to remember their own pasts. What benefits did they believe they gained from sin? Romans 6:21 is crucial because the question, "What will keep a Christian from sinning if the Law's penalties can't restrain him?" presupposes (falsely) that sin is something a sane person would desire to do.

Read aloud.

Summarize.

Questions. Question 1 points out that living "under grace" means being enslaved to obedience, righteousness, and God. The first "For Thought and Discussion" on page 96 asks you how these three slaveries are related.

Several of the optional questions deal with the place of the Old Testament Law in a Christian's life. You may prefer to postpone these until you have studied chapters 7-13, since Paul mentions this topic repeatedly.

Worship. Honor God as your Master, Husband, and Liberator from slavery to sin.

1. Bruce, *Romans,* page 145.

ROMANS 7:7-25

Law and Sin

In the course of explaining what Christ has done, Paul has said some startling things:

> *"The law was added so that the trespass might increase" (5:20).*

> *"You also died to the law. . . . For when we were controlled by the sinful nature, the sinful passions aroused by the law were at work in our bodies, so that we bore fruit for death. But now . . . we have been released from the law so that we serve in the new way of the Spirit . . ." (7:4-6).*

These statements might suggest that God's Law is "actually an evil, in some way to be identified with sin."[1] After all, if the Law were good, why would we have to die to it, and why would God have to sanctify us by grace rather than by the Law?

Therefore, Paul now more fully explains what the Law does in our lives. At the same time, he also describes what it doesn't do. Read 7:7-25, asking God to reveal the truths of this passage to you.

The Law as sin's tool (7:7-13)

1 (7:7). Paul's shift to speaking of "I" in 7:7-25 has been interpreted in various ways. The sticking point is verse 9: "Once I was alive apart from law." Does Paul mean that he was once spiritu-

103

ally alive? Most interpreters say "no" because of Psalm 51:5, 58:3, and related passages. Does he mean that his pride in his ability to please God was once alive (as a child) before he faced the full rigors of the Law?[2] Or, that he was once alive before he was responsible to keep the Law?[3] Or, that he is identifying with Adam (who was once spiritually alive apart from the Law)? Or finally, is Paul speaking of the time—literal or symbolic—when he and each person first confronts God's will and rebels?[4]

There is general agreement that in 7:7-13, Paul is describing his own and all people's experience. Some interpreters feel that this paragraph portrays only the nonChristian's situation. Others say that 7:7-13 is also part of the Christian's struggle described in 7:14-25.

1. What does Paul say about the Law in 7:7,12?

_____

_____

_____

_____

Do not covet (7:7). The Tenth Commandment (Exodus 20:17). The Ten Commandments are the core of the Law (Romans 13:8-10). Jesus summarizes them into two Great Commandments in Mark 12:28-31, and He preaches on them in Matthew 5:17-30, 12:1-14, 15:1-9, 19:16-24.

Life (7:10). God gave His Law to show His people how life could be lived joyfully and richly. If a person could keep the Law, it would give him true life (Leviticus 18:5). However, God knew that the Law would have the opposite effect upon sinful people.

2. In 7:7-11, Paul proves his conclusion in 7:12. He explains what happened when he received

104

the commandment, "Do not covet." List the series of things Paul experienced.

_____

_____

_____

_____

_____

_____

_____

_____

3. Were these effects of the Law the fault of the Law or of something else? Why?

_____

_____

_____

_____

_____

4. Why were these evil effects of the Law ultimately good for Paul (7:13)?

_____

_____

_____

_____

_____

For Thought and Discussion: According to 7:7-13, why was God's holy Law unable to make Paul righteous before God?

For Thought and Discussion: How do young children respond to commands not to do things? Do they react as in 7:8?

For Thought and Discussion: To what extent does 7:7-11 describe your past experience when you learned that coveting, theft, lust, or some other sin was wrong?

For Thought and Discussion: Can sin abuse the commandments in a Christian's life as 7:7-11 describes? Why or why not? Have you experienced 7:7-11 since becoming a Christian?

The Law in the struggle against sin
(7:14-25)

When the Law finally showed Paul how sinful sin was and how dead he was, Paul was ready to receive the gospel of justification by grace through faith.

Now his relationship to both the Law and sin is different. Notice the present tense in 7:14-25, as opposed to the past tense in 7:7-13.

5. Before Paul recognized sin as sin, he coveted without resisting (7:8-11).

    a. In what ways is he different now that he belongs to Christ and is a slave of righteousness (7:14-25)?

    _____

    _____

    _____

    _____

    _____

    _____

    _____

    b. What aspects of his pre-Christian past persist in his Christian present (7:14-25)?

    _____

    _____

    _____

    _____

    _____

    _____

    _____

Law (7:21-23). Paul uses the word in several ways here. In 7:21, he means "principle," as in 3:27. In 7:22, he means God's Law. In 7:23, "the law of my mind" is God's Law, while "another law" and "the law of sin" are principles or forces opposed to God's Law.

6. In what way is the Christian not a slave of God's Law (6:14, 7:1-6), and in what way is he a slave of God's Law (7:6,16,21-25)?

not a slave _____

_____

_____

_____

_____

still a slave _____

_____

_____

_____

_____

_____

For Further Study: Recall how in one sense the Christian is not a slave to sin (6:1-23), and in another sense he is still a slave to sin (7:25).

For Thought and Discussion: Why does a Christian commit sins even though God, not sin, is now his master?

7. Do you experience the struggle Paul discusses in 7:14-25? If so, describe one specific experience you have had of this struggle. If not, explain why you think you do not experience it.

_____

_____

_____

_____

_____

_____

Body of death (7:24). Possibly the old self, the body of sin (6:6), the sinful nature, the "flesh" which hangs onto Paul like a corpse.[5] Or, possibly life in Paul's current body, still encumbered by the sinful nature and so still destined for physical

107

Optional Application: Thank God for providing the way of escape in your struggle against sin (Romans 7:25, 1 Corinthians 10:13)—temporary escape by winning the daily battles and ultimate escape when you die physically. Thank Him for helping you accept that you will always have this struggle on earth, and for giving you hope of ultimate victory. Memorize 7:24-25, and let these verses encourage you the next time you struggle against sin.

death.[6] Or, this mass (body) of death, this deathly weight of sin against which Paul struggles.[7]

---

8. What hope does Paul have of deliverance from his struggle against sin in this life (7:24-25)? Explain in your own words.

_____

_____

_____

_____

_____

9. In 8:3, Paul speaks of "what the law was powerless to do." What was the Law powerless to do for Paul—both before and after he became a Christian—and why was it powerless (7:7-25)? See especially 7:10,15-18.

_____

_____

_____

_____

_____

_____

10. What truth in 7:7-25 seems most significant to you in your current circumstances?

_____

_____

_____

_____

108

11. How should knowing this truth affect your prayers, thoughts, and actions this week?

_____

_____

_____

_____

_____

_____

12. List any questions you have about 7:7-25.

_____

_____

_____

_____

_____

For Further Study: Outline 6:1-7:25. Add this section to your outline of Romans.

For the group

Warm-up. Ask, "Think of a recent time when you had to struggle against temptation to sin. How did the experience feel?" This question may help the group identify with Paul's experience.

By this time, your group should know each other well enough to be open about a question like this. If you sense reluctance to share more than petty struggles, set an example by sharing a real battle of your own. A leader needs to model trust. However, you will have to judge how much openness your group can handle. Don't reveal some shocking secret that will merely make the group gossip or lose respect for you. Find a way to make it clear gently that you won't accept a refusal to be honest and vulnerable in the group.

Questions. Interpretations of 7:7-25 abound. Since it is impossible for a study guide to remain utterly neutral, you may need to let group members explain how and why they differ with the view implied in this lesson. If necessary, you can have an excellent discussion about why you disagree with the guide if you insist that everyone explain his or her reasoning and control strong feelings.

Cut short the discussion of interpretations in order to allow time for sharing applications. Don't let the group stay on a purely theoretical level. Draw members to examine how the passage should affect *their* thoughts and actions.

Worship. Thank God for giving you His commandments. Thank Him for understanding your struggles to obey and for providing Jesus your Rescuer. Pray for each other in your battles against sin.

Other Views of 7:14-25

Not everyone agrees that Romans 7:14-25 describes the normal struggle of the Christian life. Two other interpretations have been popular over the centuries:

1. *Paul is speaking of the nonChristian life.* In support of this view are:
   a. phrases like "sold as a slave to sin" (7:14), "I know that nothing good lives in me" (7:18), and "What a wretched man I am!" (7:24)—these do not seem to describe Christian life;
   b. the contrast between chapters 7 and 8;
   c. the problem that faith in Christ seems pointless if it leads to spiritual misery.
   Against these arguments, it is said that:
   a. Paul uses the present tense throughout 7:14-25;
   b. Paul means that he is now a struggling slave of sin in part of himself, as opposed to a passive slave of sin in his entirety;
   c. Paul says only that there is nothing good "in my sinful nature" (7:18), but does not deny that the Holy Spirit is in him (8:9-10);
   d. Christians engaged in fierce struggle against sin do at times feel wretched. Earthly life is wretched compared to resurrection life, but Paul does not wallow in

(continued on page 111)

(continued from page 110)

despair in 7:25; on the contrary, 7:25 could not be said by an unbeliever.

2. *Paul is speaking of a substandard Christian life.* The "I" of these verses is an "unspiritual" or "carnal" (7:14) Christian, in contrast to the spiritual Christian described in 8:1-17. The chief argument here is that 7:14-25 is incompatible with Paul's account of the believer's freedom from sin and his victory in the Spirit (6:6,14,17-18,22; 8:2-11).
Against this view are:
a. the present tense in 7:14-25;
b. Paul's repetition of his current struggle immediately *after* his joyful statement of thanks (7:25); the thanksgiving and the struggle seem to be part of the same present time;
c. the testimony of most Christians. "Unspiritual" ("carnal" in KJV) in 7:14 means "not fully spiritual," or "not fully sanctified." No Christian can claim to have attained perfect holiness in this life. Saints from Augustine to Luther to many moderns have acknowledged 7:14-25 as their present experience.[8]

1. Cranfield, page 154.
2. Murray, page 251; *The NIV Study Bible,* page 1715.
3. According to Jewish tradition, a person is not fully accountable to keep the Law until he or she reaches the age of responsibility, about thirteen years of age. At that point, a boy becomes *bar mitzvah,* a "son of the commandment," and a girl becomes *bas mitzvah,* a "daughter of the commandment." See Bruce, *Romans,* pages 147-148.
4. Cranfield, pages 156, 159-161.
5. *The NIV Study Bible,* page 1716.
6. Cranfield, page 169; Murray, pages 268-269.
7. Hodge, page 238.
8. Hodge, page 229; Cranfield, pages 156-158; Murray, pages 256-259; *The NIV Study Bible,* page 1716.

ROMANS 8:1-17

Life in the Spirit

In chapter 6, Paul explained *why* a Christian wants not to sin even though Christ has taken all the penalties. However, Paul's advice on *how* a Christian can avoid sinning was: "count yourselves dead to sin but alive to God" (6:11); "do not let sin reign in your mortal body" (6:12); and "do not offer the parts of your body to sin . . . but rather . . . to God" (6:13). All this counting, not letting, and not offering might sound as though life under grace is much like life under law—we acquire the holy character God desires by sheer effort of our wills.

But then Paul explained how we died to the Law as well as to sin (7:1-6). Because we were sinful, the Law brought us death, not life (7:7-13). Therefore, we had to die to the Law through Christ. Having died to the Law's penalty of death, we now find we fervently desire to keep God's Law, but we are unable to do so because our sin nature persists in us (7:14-25). How, then, can we become holy and righteous in our characters?

Chapter 7 makes it clear that we cannot by willpower obey 6:11-13 or keep the Law we delight in. Read 7:4-6 and 8:1-17 for God's solution.

For Further Study:
How does being baptized into Christ's death and united with Him in His life (6:1-14) enable us not to sin?

No condemnation (8:1-4)

Condemnation (8:1). Penal servitude, imprisonment. Not just the legal status, "guilty," but also the punishment after the sentence.[1]

For Thought and Discussion: What is "the law of the Spirit of life" (8:2)?

1. How does Paul describe the Christian's life in the following verses?

7:4-6 _____

_____

7:14-25 _____

_____

8:1-2 _____

_____

Law (8:2-3). In 8:2, the word means a controlling power in each case (compare 7:23). In 8:3, it means God's Law in the Old Testament, which is also a power in a way, since it can produce life or death, justification or condemnation.

Likeness of sinful man (8:3). "Christ in his incarnation became truly a man, but, unlike all other men, was sinless."[2] However, at the end He took our sin upon Himself in order to die in our place (2 Corinthians 5:21).

To be a sin offering (8:3). Or, "for sin." The Greek translation of the Old Testament (the Septuagint) always used these words to render the Hebrew for "sin offering" (Leviticus 4:3), and once for "guilt offering" (Isaiah 53:10).[3]

Condemned (8:3). As in 8:1, the word means not just sentenced to death but also put to death.

---

2. The written Law of the Old Testament is powerless to enable us to obey God or attain life (7:10,15-18)—it cannot free us from sin and death. However, how has God done what the Law is powerless to do (8:2-3)?

_____

_____

_____

114

_____

_____

_____

3. What is God's goal in releasing us from the law of sin and death (8:4; compare 7:4)?

_____

_____

_____

_____

_____

Flesh or Spirit (8:5-11)

4. In 8:5-8, Paul contrasts the way of life "according to the Spirit" with the way of life "according to the flesh" (NASB). List as many contrasts as you can find.

Spirit	flesh

For Thought and Discussion: According to 7:4 and 8:4, what place does God's Law have in our lives?

For Thought and Discussion: Is the path to holiness a daily process or a one-time victory? Support your answer from Romans 8:5-13 and Luke 9:23.

For Thought and Discussion: What difference should our hope of ultimate resurrection, both physical and spiritual (8:11), make to our lives now?

Optional Application: Meditate on your freedom from condemnation, sin, and death (8:1-2). How does this affect your attitude toward your circumstances? How can you reflect this attitude in your prayers and actions this week?

Optional Application: Thank God for killing sin by sacrificing His Son (8:3). Thank Him for giving His Spirit to make you holy. Ask Him to make you increasingly aware this week of the Spirit's availability to help you resist sin.

Optional Application: Make a list of the struggles with sin that you are currently facing. Toward what is the flesh pulling you? Toward what is the Spirit guiding you? Ask God to help you focus your mind on the desires of the Spirit. Thank Him that He will help you, and act in faith.

For Thought and Discussion: a. What does Paul call the Holy Spirit in 8:9-11?
b. What can we learn about the three Persons of the Trinity from these names?
c. What parts do the Father, the Son, and the Spirit each play in making us holy (8:1-11)?

5. What do you think it means to "have their minds set on" (to "mind" in KJV) the flesh or the Spirit (8:5-7)?

_____

_____

_____

_____

_____

_____

Controlled by (8:8-9). Literally, "in" the flesh or "in" the Spirit (KJV, NASB). To be "in" the flesh or the Spirit means to be united with, directed toward, and impelled by one or the other. It means to be controlled, but not in the extreme sense of loss of free will.

6. Is the directing power of the Spirit available only to some Christians (8:9)? Why or why not?

_____

_____

_____

_____

_____

7. If the Spirit is in you, what else is true of you . . .

now (8:10)? _____

_____

_____

_____

_____

in the future (8:11)? _____

_____

_____

_____

_____

Put to death (8:12-13)

In 8:12-13, "Therefore" looks back to 8:1-11, and "For" points to a reason in 8:13.

8. What obligation does Paul imply we *do* have (8:12)?

_____

_____

_____

_____

9. Why do we have this obligation (8:1-11,13)?

_____

_____

_____

_____

_____

_____

_____

10. What does it mean to "put to death the misdeeds of the body" (8:13)? Explain in your own words.

_____

_____

_____

For Thought and Discussion: How is 6:12-14,19 related to 8:5,13?

For Thought and Discussion: How is putting misdeeds to death different from trying to keep the Law by force of effort alone (7:6; 8:2-4,6,13)?

Optional Application: In what area of your life do you need to put the deeds of the body to death and set your mind on the desires of the Spirit (8:5,13)? What can you do and pray to accomplish this? What attitudes toward your power and God's do you need?

117

_____

_____

_____

Children of God (8:14-17)

Abba (8:15). An affectionate, intimate Aramaic word for "Father," comparable to "Papa." Jews did not use this term for God, but Jesus used it (Mark 14:36) and apparently encouraged His disciples to do so. See Luke 11:2, Galatians 4:6.

---

11. Romans 8:15-16 tells what is true of us if we are led and indwelt by the Spirit. Think of the implications for our lives. What sorts of attitudes and actions will follow if we are calling God "Abba, Father" sincerely?

_____

_____

_____

_____

_____

_____

12. Summarize what Paul has said in 8:1-17 about how we can win the battles of 7:14-25, how we can increasingly fulfill the righteous requirements of the Law (8:4).

_____

_____

_____

_____

118

13. What one truth from 8:1-17 would you like to focus on for application this week?

_____

_____

_____

_____

_____

14. With what prayer, meditation, and/or action can you put this truth into practice?

_____

_____

_____

_____

_____

15. List any questions you have about 8:1-17.

_____

_____

_____

For the group

Warm-up. Think of one time during the past week when you have experienced the Holy Spirit's guidance.

Questions. Questions 1-3 ask you to relate chapter 8 to chapter 7. It's essential to make connections like this when you are studying a systematic book like Romans.

On questions 4-6, discuss practical ways in which you each need to set your minds on the Spirit. Share some experiences of being drawn to set your minds on the flesh, and some strategies for disciplining yourselves to set your minds on the Spirit. Discuss what "the flesh" means to Paul.

Questions 8-12 can also lead to a lengthy discussion of applications. How does your adoption affect your behavior?

Chapter 8 is a tough but crucial passage. You may want to take more than two weeks for lessons eleven and twelve.

Worship. Thank God for setting you free from the law of sin and death, and for determining to fulfill in you the righteous requirements of the law of the Spirit. Thank Him for putting His Spirit in you, so that you can set your mind on Him and live. Thank God for adopting you as sons and heirs, and for promising to give life to your bodies. Praise God as "Abba, Father." Ask Him to help you obey Him as Father and to share in Christ's sufferings.

Flesh and Spirit

The Greek words *sarx* and *pneuma* are central to Paul's teaching in Romans, but they are not easy to understand. In fact, while KJV and NASB follow the traditional rendering of *sarx* as "flesh" in all cases, the NIV and other modern versions use various English words to convey the various senses of *sarx*. The NIV uses "body," "mankind," "people," "human," and "sinful nature" to render *sarx* in Romans. Thus, the NIV tells us what Paul means by *sarx* in any given verse, whereas KJV and NASB allow us to decide.

Scholars debate what Paul means by *sarx* in particular passages, but all agree that he does not think of it as the pagan Greeks did. Since Greek philosophy focused on man, the Greeks thought of "flesh" versus "soul" as distinct parts of a man. The flesh was considered the corrupt, mortal prison of the pure, immortal soul. The soul was good, the body evil. By contrast, Paul adopts the Old Testament idea of flesh. The Old Testament focuses on God, so it contrasts "flesh" and "spirit" (Isaiah 31:3). "Flesh" is the substance of human and animal life; hence, it is mortal, transient, and weak compared to "spirit," which is the power and vitality of God. This is the contrast we see in Paul's writings: (human) flesh versus (divine) Spirit or (God-centered human) spirit, not (human) flesh versus (human) soul.[4]

(continued on page 121)

(continued from page 120)

More specifically, Paul uses "flesh" in the following ways:

1. *Body.* The human body in a morally neutral sense. In Romans 2:28, "physical" (NIV) is literally "in the flesh" (NASB). (See also Galatians 2:20; Philippians 1:22,24.)

2. *Mankind.* Again, morally neutral. In Romans 3:20, "no one" (NIV) is literally, "no flesh" (KJV).

3. *Human nature as weak,* either physically, intellectually (Romans 6:19), or emotionally. This is less neutral than (1) or (2).

4. *Human nature as earthly rather than divine.* That is, not bad in itself, but inferior to the things of the Spirit. This includes:

a. *biological relationship.* Where we would speak of "blood" relatives, Paul writes of descent "according to the flesh" (KJV). Christ's physical descent from David (Romans 1:3-4) is important, but less important than His divine Sonship by the Holy Spirit. Likewise, the Jews' descent from Abraham (9:3,5,8) is not sinful, but it is less ultimately decisive than the elect's status as Abraham's spiritual offspring (9:8).

b. *things of the world.* The wisdom "after the flesh" (1 Corinthians 1:26, KJV)—expertise in human endeavors like rhetoric, literature, and technology—is not necessarily evil but is far inferior to God's wisdom about spiritual things. (Compare "wisdom of this world" in 1 Corinthians 2:6.) Fleshly ways of warfare (2 Corinthians 10:2-4) are irrelevant in the important battles of the spirit.

5. *Human nature as sinful.* To be fleshly or human is evil when man focuses on the fleshly realm and desires, sees everything by fleshly standards ("according to the flesh," KJV), and rejects the authority and perspective of God's Spirit. This includes:

a. *unregenerate human nature.* Before accepting Christ, every person is "in the flesh" in this sense (Romans 7:5, 8:8-9), wholly given to his human, self-centered aims and against God's plans.

(continued on page 122)

(continued from page 121)

b. *the old nature that persists in the believer.* Although the believer's flesh has been crucified, it continues to have a sinful influence (7:18). Therefore, the believer must strive "by the Spirit" not to live according to the habits and outlook of unregenerate human nature (8:4-7,12-14). The Christian has the Spirit's power to choose not to act according to the flesh, but rather to act in accord with God's aims.[5]

The difficulty with interpreting *pneuma* is different. The Greek word itself is never capitalized, so only context and grammar[6] can tell us when to translate it as "Spirit" and when "spirit." Normally, *pneuma* in Romans means one of the following:

1. *The Holy Spirit of God.* We can learn a great deal about the Third Person of the Trinity from Romans (5:5, 8:1-27, 9:1, 15:19).

2. *The "spiritual" part of man,* the part that enables him to relate to God, who is Spirit (Romans 1:9, 8:16, 12:11). Man's spirit is dead or asleep until it is enlivened by the Holy Spirit. (See also 1 Corinthians 2:14-3:1, 15:44-46.)[7]

1. Bruce, *Romans,* page 159; Cranfield, pages 177-178; Stuart Olyott, *The Gospel as it Really is: Paul's Epistle to the Romans Simply Explained* (Hertfordshire, England: Evangelical Press, 1979), page 71.
2. *The NIV Study Bible,* page 1716.
3. Bruce, *Romans,* page 161.
4. It is worth noting that the "works of the flesh" (KJV) in Galatians 5:19-21 include sins of the mind as well as the body. Also, the Christian's body is indwelt by the Holy Spirit (Romans 8:11, 1 Corinthians 6:19-20), offered as a sacrifice to God (Romans 12:1), and destined to be glorified (Romans 8:23, Philippians 3:21). These passages make it clear that Paul does not consider the body evil while the mind or soul is good.
5. Bruce, *Romans,* pages 40-46; Horst Seebass and Anthony C. Thiselton, "Flesh," *The New International Dictionary of New Testament Theology,* volume 1, pages 671-682.
6. The word *pneuma* is neuter in Greek. However, the New Testament writers use masculine articles ("the") and pronouns ("He") when speaking of the Holy Spirit to show that He is a person.
7. Bruce, *Romans,* pages 46-52; Eberhard Kamlah and Colin Brown, "Spirit," *The New International Dictionary of New Testament Theology,* volume 3, pages 689-708.

ROMANS 8:17-39

Certainty

Putting to death the deeds of the flesh and setting the mind on the desires of the Spirit means nothing less than sharing in Christ's sufferings (8:17). On top of that, we have to face the normal afflictions of human life—health, money, work, people, and so on. What is Paul's perspective on our plight? Read 8:17-39.

1. Make a quick list of everything Paul says in 8:11-27 that the Spirit does or demonstrates.

   8:2 _____

   _____

   8:6 _____

   _____

   8:11 _____

   _____

   8:13 _____

   _____

   8:14-16 _____

   _____

   _____

   _____

8:23 _____

_____

_____

_____

8:26-27 _____

_____

_____

_____

Future glory (8:17-25)

If indeed (8:17). This phrase does not imply that our
   suffering is a condition for attaining glory, since
   Christ's suffering assures us of glory. Instead,
   the phrase means that sharing Christ's suffering
   points toward, and is evidence of, sharing His
   glory. Present suffering does not contradict
   future glory.

2. Why is sharing Christ's sufferings worth the
   pain (8:17-18)?

_____

_____

_____

_____

Frustration (8:20). "Vanity" or "futility." When
   Adam sinned, God announced the inevitable
   consequences: the ground that Adam would
   have to cultivate was cursed (Genesis 3:17-19).
   The creation was meant to glorify God, but it
   could not do this perfectly as long as mankind,
   to whom God gave dominion over the creation
   (Genesis 1:28), was not perfectly glorifying God.
   Therefore, the creation is frustrated, unable to
   fulfill its purpose. However, God did not leave it
   without hope of redemption through a descendant of Eve (Genesis 3:15).[1]

124

3. The creation is waiting, frustrated but with hope, for something to happen. What is it waiting for (8:19-22)?

_____

_____

_____

_____

_____

4. In one sense, we have already been adopted as God's children and heirs (8:15-16), but in another sense, our adoption has not been fulfilled. The Spirit is the pledge, guarantee, and down payment of our adoption (8:15-16,23).

   What will happen when our adoption is fully realized (8:11,23)? (*Optional:* See 1 Corinthians 15:35-44.)

_____

_____

_____

_____

_____

_____

Intercession (8:26-27)

5. Hope of glory sustains us in the midst of suffering and frustration (8:17-25). Another support we have is the Holy Spirit. How is His aid in 8:26-27 an enormous help to us?

_____

_____

_____

_____

_____

For Further Study: On question 4, see 2 Corinthians 5:1-10 and Philippians 3:20-21.

For Thought and Discussion: Why is it significant that our *bodies*, not just our disembodied souls or spirits, will be redeemed?

For Thought and Discussion: Recall the meaning of "hope" from 5:2,4-5 (page 77). Why do you think God saved us "in this hope," rather than giving us our full inheritance of resurrection glory immediately (8:24-25)? Consider what waiting in hope accomplishes in us.

125

Optional Application: a. Think about your present status with God and the Spirit you have as a down payment. Then think about your hope. What specific areas of your life can your hope and down payment help you deal with patiently? Specifically how does your hope affect your attitude toward those circumstances?
b. Meditate on 8:17-25 this week.

For Thought and Discussion: Are you aware of the Spirit doing in you what 8:26-27 describes? How is this promise a comfort to you?

For Further Study: Read part or all of 8:28-39 aloud with feeling. Listen to God's promises.

6. Summarize what Paul says in 8:17-27.

_____

_____

_____

_____

_____

God's sovereignty (8:28-30)

Paul has been discussing how we become holy, how we acquire the righteous character that conforms to the status we received when we were justified. He has acknowledged that this process of sanctification (being made holy) will be a long struggle full of suffering (7:14-25; 8:5,10,12-13,17-27). However, he has encouraged us with the knowledge that hope of sharing Christ's glory lies at the end of our path, and the Spirit is in us praying and empowering us all along it.

Now Paul reaches the climax of his teaching on sanctification.

7. How does 8:28 encourage you as you face suffering and the struggle against sin?

_____

_____

_____

_____

_____

_____

Called (8:28). Effectually called. The word assumes a positive response.[2] God loved and called us not only before we became perfectly holy but even before we were declared righteous.

126

Foreknew (8:29). Many people think Paul intends the kind of knowing in Genesis 18:19, Jeremiah 1:5, Amos 3:2—a knowing that implies choosing by grace.[3] Others note that in Genesis 4:1 and Hosea 13:5, "know" suggests the intimate knowledge of a marriage relationship.[4] However, others feel that Paul means no more than "that in eternity past God knew those who by faith would become His people."[5]

Predestined (8:29-30). To appoint beforehand. See Romans 9:1-11:36 and Ephesians 1:4-12.

For Further Study: See the words *know* and *foreknow* in John 10:14-15, 1 Corinthians 8:3, Galatians 4:9, 2 Timothy 2:19, and 1 Peter 1:20. You can also look these words up in a concordance.

8. To what has God predestined us? What is God's purpose in choosing us (Romans 8:29, Ephesians 1:11-12)?

_____

_____

_____

_____

_____

_____

For Thought and Discussion: In what two ways does Paul describe us in 8:28? Why is each significant?

Glorified (8:30). Our future glory is so certain that Paul can speak of it as an accomplished fact in the past tense. Paul does not mention sanctification, partly because he has been speaking of glory (8:17-18,21,23,29) and possibly because "Sanctification is glory begun; glory is sanctification completed."[6]

Study Skill—Defining Words
Sometimes a word in the Bible has a richer or more precise meaning than it has in everyday speech. Sometimes the Greek or Hebrew original means something slightly different from what we think the English word means. You can use study aids to discover these

(continued on page 128)

(continued from page 127)

For Further Study:
Give a brief definition in your own words of what it means that God (8:29-30) . . .
foreknew you,
predestined you,
called you,
justified you,
has glorified and is glorifying you.

fuller meanings. An ordinary English diction-ary is often a great help. Comparing several translations of the Bible will also reveal dif-ferent shades of meaning. Bible dictionaries and encyclopedias define words and give cross-references. If you write down your own brief definition after using study aids, you will be more likely to remember what a word means when you encounter it again.

9. How is 8:29-30 an encouragement to you as you suffer and battle sin in this life?

_____

_____

_____

_____

_____

God's love (8:31-39)

10. Why can we be certain that God will give us everything necessary for our glorification (8:32)?

_____

_____

_____

_____

_____

11. How can we be sure that in God's court of law, we will be found "not guilty"?

8:31 _____

_____

_____

8:33-34a _____

_____

_____

8:34b _____

_____

_____

_____

_____

12. Christ intercedes for us and offers His own life in our place because He loves us. However, because we have pain and affliction, we might wonder whether Christ has ceased to love and intercede for us (8:35-36). How does Paul calm this doubt (8:37-39)?

_____

_____

_____

_____

Your response

13. Reread 8:17-39. What one truth from this passage would you like to take to heart and apply this week?

_____

_____

_____

_____

_____

_____

_____

For Thought and Discussion: What does 8:28-39 reveal about God's and Christ's will, character, and attributes?

Optional Application: For the next week, meditate and pray about what God has predestined you to be (8:29). Ask Him to give you a fervent desire for this to happen and a peaceful faith that He can accomplish it. Ask Him to show you how you can cooperate with this purpose. Memorize 8:29.

Optional Application: Do your circumstances tempt you to doubt God's love or control in your life? If so, choose verses from 8:28-39 to memorize, meditate on, and pray about. Ask God to enable this passage to change your attitude. How can your actions and words reflect these truths about God?

For Further Study: Outline 8:1-39. The subtitles in lessons eleven and twelve may help you.

14. How would you like this truth to affect your attitudes and actions? What action can you take to help accomplish this by the Spirit's power?

_____

_____

_____

_____

_____

_____

15. Summarize 8:1-39.

_____

_____

_____

_____

_____

16. You have now finished the second main section of Paul's explanation of the gospel. If you are not already working on an outline, use this space to outline 6:1-8:39. Think of a title for the whole section, then divide the section into logical units and give them titles.

_____

_____

_____

_____

_____

_____

_____

_____

_____

_____

_____

_____

17. Write down any questions you have about
    8:17-39.

_____

_____

_____

_____

For the group

Warm-up. Ask, "What do you hope for? How certain
are you of that hope?" Many people think hope is
like wishing for something that is almost too good
to be true. In Greek, hope is confidence in a
certainty.

Questions. It might be helpful to make three lists
showing what the Father, the Son, and the Spirit
each does in our lives. Romans 8 tells us a great
deal about the Trinity. In your worship time, praise
the Triune God for the things you have listed.

Predestination is a major issue for many people. You may want to postpone any discussion of it
until lesson thirteen, fourteen, or fifteen, since Paul
unfolds his teaching on predestination more fully in
9:1-11:36. Some books on this subject are: Martin
Luther's *The Bondage of the Will,* John Calvin's
Institutes (the chapter on predestination), and Ste-
phen Charnock's *The Being and Attributes of God*
(chapters on God's wisdom and knowledge).

Focus on the nature of God in 8:28-39. What
are His goals for us? How can we be certain that He
will accomplish them? How does the passage reflect
God's love, faithfulness, power, etc.? How do these
guarantees affect our lives? In your worship time,
praise God for His attributes as revealed in 8:28-39.

Application. Briefly report on the results of your applications during the last couple of weeks. Can you see God at work in your lives? If not, don't despair; it often takes time for fruit to become visible. Plan to pray for each other now or at the end of your meeting.

Worship. Thank God for the hope He promises and guarantees to you. Praise Him for His purposes to conform you to Jesus and glorify you. Praise His unfailing love and His faithfulness to keep His promises. Thank the Spirit who intercedes for you.

1. Cranfield, page 196; *The NIV Study Bible*, page 1717.
2. Hodge, pages 280-281; *The NIV Study Bible*, page 1718.
3. Bruce, *Romans*, page 177; Cranfield, page 205; John Stott, *Men Made New: an exposition of Romans 5-8* (Chicago: Inter-Varsity Press, 1966), page 101; Hodge, page 284.
4. Olyott, page 80.
5. *The NIV Study Bible*, page 1718.
6. Bruce, *Romans*, page 178.

ROMANS 9:1-29

Israel

Paul has shown that:

1. All people have sinned, but they can be reconciled to God by faith in the gracious death of Jesus (1:18-5:21);

2. God wants His justified ones to conform to the likeness of His Son and thereby fulfill the righteous requirements of the Law (8:4,29), but this is only possible by the power of the Holy Spirit (6:1-8:39).

Now Paul turns to a matter that concerns him deeply, the problem of the unbelieving Jews. In light of God's promises to the Jewish people, why does it seem that God has rejected them? What place do they have in His plan of salvation? This may seem a minor point to us, but in fact it raises crucial questions about God's character.

Jesus is humanly a Jew (1:2-3), and the gospel is God's saving power "first for the Jew" (1:16). God called the Jews with an "everlasting covenant" (Genesis 17:7-8,13,19; Deuteronomy 7:6-10; Isaiah 41:8-16, 43:1-7; Jeremiah 31:3-4). Our confidence about our salvation depends on God's sovereign foreknowledge, calling, and promises (Romans 8:28-30). If God has rejected the Jews, we might question whether our confidence is valid. We might doubt God's Word, His justice, His foreknowledge, His gifts, and His call (Romans 9:6,14,19,21; 11:2,29). Therefore, Paul takes three chapters to clarify the Jews' status.

Paul's reasoning in 9:1-11:36 is a unit, so you will benefit from reading all of it again now. (If your

For Further Study: If you didn't write titles for chapters 9-11 on pages 17-18, or if you would like to make new ones, write titles for the following five subsections:

9:1-29
9:30-10:21
11:1-10
11:11-32
11:33-36

time is limited, read just 9:1-29.) If you wrote titles for 9:1-11:36 on page 133, look back at them. Look also at the outlines on page 24.

Paul's grief (9:1-5)

1. How does Paul feel about the fact that most of his fellow Jews have rejected Christ and so face eternal separation from God (9:1-3)?

For Thought and Discussion: Reread the list of Israel's blessings in Romans 9:4-5.
   a. Why are the Law and Temple worship as great blessings as the adoption, glory, covenants, and promises?
   b. What is Israel's greatest blessing (9:5)? Why is this the nation's greatest blessing?

For Thought and Discussion: What does Paul affirm about Jesus in 9:5?

_____

_____

_____

_____

People of Israel (9:4). The descendants of Jacob (whom God renamed "Israel"; see Genesis 32:28). The titles "Israel" and "Israelite" signified to the Jews that they were God's chosen people.[1]

Adoption (9:4). God adopted the nation Israel as His son (Exodus 4:22-23, Jeremiah 31:9, Hosea 11:1).

Glory (9:4). God manifested His presence with His people in the form of a radiant cloud that was nearly impossible to look at (Exodus 16:7,10; 40:34-35; Ezekiel 1:28).

Covenants (9:4). In particular, God made royal treaties or pacts with Abraham (Genesis 15:1-21, 17:1-14); with Israel at Mount Sinai (Exodus 19:5, 24:1-4), on the plains of Moab (Deuteronomy 29:1-15), and at Mounts Gerizim and Ebal (Joshua 8:30-35); and with David (2 Samuel 23:5; Psalm 89:3-4, 132:11-12).

Promises (9:4). God promised land, descendants, and His own presence to Abraham, Isaac, Jacob, and Jacob's sons. God promised salvation, peace, the Messiah, and the restoration of the nation to all Israel through the prophets.

Patriarchs (9:5). Literally, "fathers." That is, Abraham, Isaac, Jacob, Jacob's twelve sons, and possibly other Old Testament people such as David (Mark 11:10, Acts 2:29).

God's past practice (9:6-13)

Because Paul's topic in 9:1-11:36 is the Jews, he cites the Old Testament—God's Word to Israel—frequently. Unless you are very familiar with the Old Testament, you would benefit from reading the references in context for yourself, to see if you agree with the summary explanations in this study guide.

Through Isaac (9:7). To prove that God's Old Testament promises to Israel have not failed, Paul cites two Old Testament instances in which He acted much like He is acting toward the Jews today. The first instance is the case of Isaac versus Ishmael.

Both men were Abraham's biological sons, and both were circumcized members of the covenant family. But God ordained that only Isaac would inherit the promise of descendants who would possess the land of Canaan and become a blessing to all the nations (Genesis 12:1-3, 15:18-21, 17:19-21). God did not reject Ishmael personally (Scripture says nothing about his personal salvation); God simply declared that Ishmael's descendants would be Gentiles outside the chosen nation (Genesis 16:7-14, 17:20). This was not an act of cruelty, for God's ultimate goal in choosing Isaac was to bless the descendants of both men through Christ.

Rebekah's children (Romans 9:10). A Jew could argue that Ishmael was rejected not because of God's sovereign and merciful will, but because Ishmael's mother was a slave. Therefore, Paul adds the case of Jacob and Esau, who were born to the same parents within minutes of each other. Paul stresses that God chose Jacob to inherit before either boy had a chance to do good or show faith (Genesis 25:19-26). ***Loved*** and ***hated*** in Romans 9:13 mean "chose" and

135

For Thought and Discussion: What can we learn about God's character from Romans 9:1-13 and His treatment of Abraham's children and grandchildren?

Optional Application: How could you acquire and show an attitude toward others' salvation like the attitude Paul describes in 9:1-3? Talk to God about this.

Optional Application: What implications do God's character and His dealings with Israel have for your life?

"rejected."[2] Again, the purpose of Esau's rejection was so that ultimately his descendants could be saved through Jacob's descendant, Jesus.

2. What principle has characterized God's dealings with His people ever since Abraham (Romans 9:6-8)?

_____

_____

_____

_____

3. Why is it significant that God chose Jacob before either he or Esau had done good or bad (9:11-12)?

_____

_____

_____

_____

_____

4. What is God's "purpose in election" (9:11)? That is, what is His ultimate goal in electing some of Abraham's biological children but setting others aside?

_____

_____

_____

_____

Sovereign mercy (9:14-29)

Paul has established the principle that throughout Old Testament history, God continually chose a group within Israel who inherited the promises given to the whole nation. However, this selection raises another question: Has God been practicing unjust discrimination all along?

5. Why would 9:6-13 suggest that God is unjust (9:14)? For instance, see 9:8,11,13.

_____

_____

_____

_____

_____

I will have mercy (9:15). Paul quotes Exodus 33:19, in which God is revealing His nature and character to Moses. (God did this repeatedly; see Exodus 3:14-15, 33:18-19, 34:5-7.)
   To "have mercy" means to go beyond justice to give someone what he doesn't deserve or not give him what he does deserve.

6. According to Romans 9:15, what are some of the essential aspects of God's character that direct His will and purpose?

_____

_____

_____

_____

7. Reread Romans 3:19-20,23-24. Does any person have a right to be chosen by God or receive His mercy? Why or why not?

_____

For Thought and Discussion: On what basis does God choose people to inherit His promises (9:16)? What factors do not affect His choice?

137

a. Decide for yourself what it means for God to harden a heart and for a person to harden his own heart. Study the examples of Pharaoh, the Israelites, and Jesus' disciples (Exodus 4:21; 8:15,19,32; 14:1-4,17,29-31; Deuteronomy 15:7-8; Joshua 11:19-20; 1 Samuel 6:6; Proverbs 28:14; Isaiah 19:19-23; 42:1,6-7; Mark 3:1-6; 6:45-52; 8:14-21).

b. Is your heart hard in any areas? How can you find out?

For Thought and Discussion: What does Romans 9:15,18 tell you about God's prerogatives?

Pharaoh (9:17). God chose the king of Egypt in Moses' day for a special role in His plan of salvation. It was a negative role, but still crucial. Pharaoh's refusal to free the Israelites allowed God to display His love for Israel and His saving power by sending the plagues on Egypt and parting the Red Sea (Exodus 5:1-14:31). Pharaoh's hardness made possible Israel's faith (Exodus 14:31).

Hardens (9:18). A hard heart is one closed to knowing that God is present, resistant to being vulnerable to God, and unable to hear and obey God. The Scripture speaks of God hardening people's hearts and of those same people hardening their own hearts. This is at the core of the mystery of predestination and human choice.

8. God selected this man to be Pharaoh and hardened his heart against Israel (9:18). In your own words, explain God's purposes for doing this (9:17).

9. Someone might object that a person cannot be blamed if God hardens his heart (9:18-19). Why is this objection wrong, in view of God's status

138

and character (9:15,20-21)? Consider your answers to questions 6 through 8.

_____

_____

_____

_____

_____

_____

For Thought and Discussion: Is it sinful to ask questions of God? What attitude is Paul rebuking in 9:20?

For Thought and Discussion: According to 9:14-29, God doesn't exercise His free will arbitrarily. What purposes guide His decisions?

Objects of his wrath (9:22). Literally, "vessels of wrath" (KJV). Remember that all of us were objects of God's wrath and destined for destruction because of our deeds and nature (Romans 1:18, 2:5-6, 3:9; Ephesians 2:1-3).

10. God has been treating the objects of His wrath with great "kindness, tolerance, and patience" (2:4, 9:22).

a. Why has He been doing this (9:22-24)?

_____

_____

_____

_____

_____

_____

b. What do these facts tell you about God's character?

_____

_____

_____

139

Optional Application: Share with someone the most significant thing you learned from 9:14-29, and tell that person why this truth is so important to you.

Optional Application: a. Are you ever tempted to regard God as unfair or arbitrary in His dealings with people? If so, meditate on His sovereignty and mercy in 9:6-29, and talk to Him about your feelings. How does this chapter affect your view of God?

b. Meditate on God's sovereignty and mercy in Ephesians 1:1-14.

Optional Application: Think about how you have experienced God's mercy or patience (9:15,22-23). Look for ways to respond in gratitude.

For Further Study: You can add 9:1-29 to your outline now, or wait and do all of 9:1-11:36 at once.

Gentiles (9:24). Including the descendants of Ishmael, Esau, and Pharaoh.

Not my people (9:25). As Hosea prophesied, the ten northern tribes of Israel were conquered and dispersed among the Gentiles; their descendants became Gentiles, not Jews. However, God promised to bring them back into His chosen people (Hosea 1:10, 2:23).

Remnant (9:27). As Isaiah predicted, only a remnant of the northern nation of Israel survived destruction in 722 BC, and only a remnant of the southern nation of Judah survived conquest and exile in 586 BC. Paul sees God continuing to purge Israel and choose only a remnant.

11. In summary, why is God's constant choice of a remnant within Israel just (9:14-29)?

12. What is the most significant truth you have learned about God in 9:1-29?

140

13. What implications does this truth have for your life and your attitude toward God?

_____

_____

_____

_____

_____

_____

14. What action can you take this week regarding what you have learned?

_____

_____

_____

_____

_____

15. List any questions you have about 9:1-29.

_____

_____

_____

For the group

Warm-up. Have everyone think of someone whom he or she longs to see accept Christ. This will help the group identify with Paul in 9:1-5. Or, ask group members to think of circumstances in their lives that have tempted them to consider God unfair.

Summarize. Summarize what 9:1-29 is about and why it is important to the theme of Romans. You may want to look at an outline together.

Two views. There are several major interpretations of this section, and advocates of each tend to feel strongly about their views. Two of these are:

1. Paul's main point is that the Old Testament promises to Israel have been transferred to the elect of both Jews and Gentiles, so that those promises no longer apply to the Jews as a people.

2. Paul's point is that an elect group within the physical family of Israel continues to inherit the Old Testament promises. This does not contradict the fact that elect Gentiles also inherit those promises, but in 9:1-11:36 Paul is talking about the elect within physical Israel.

This study guide tries to remain as neutral as possible on debatable issues, but sometimes a question cannot be worded without implying one interpretation or the other. If you don't like the bias of a question, reword it to imply the other interpretation when you lead the study.

Some people object to view 2 on the grounds that it a) implies uncritical support for the modern political nation of Israel, b) impedes evangelism among Arabs and others, c) makes Gentile Christians inferior to Jewish ones, and d) suggests that salvation is based on blood relationship rather than on faith.

Other people object to view 1 on the grounds that it e) grows out of and promotes anti-Semitism, and f) suggests that God has abandoned a covenant He promised never to abandon.

Of these objections, (a), (b), (c), and (e) are not necessary implications of either view. Neither interpretation of 9:1-11:36 needs to make a person anti-Semitic, anti-Arab, nor politically pro-Israeli. Objections (d) and (f) are more serious, so you should look for solutions in the passage itself. For discussions of each view, see C. E. B. Cranfield's *Shorter Commentary on Romans* and Stuart Olyott's *The Gospel as It Really Is: the Epistle to the Romans Simply Explained.*

142

Sovereign mercy. Have someone briefly tell the story of the Exodus, including why it was necessary to raise up a hard-hearted Pharaoh. If necessary, the group leader should read Exodus 5:1-15:21 as background. In Romans 9:14-29, Paul assumes that his readers know this story in detail, so he doesn't bother to remind them.

Romans 9:6-29 emphasizes God's sovereignty, His power and freedom to do whatever He likes. Many people find this idea depressing or even threatening at first glance; a Sovereign God seems like a capricious tyrant. If your group feels this way, draw attention to the repeated word *mercy* in this passage. Recall God's sovereign acts of mercy in 1:18-8:39. Point out that Paul doesn't say that God arbitrarily condemns innocent people, but that He mercifully saves guilty ones.

Discuss your feelings about God. Does His unlimited power make you uncomfortable? If so, do you know why? People who grew up with harsh fathers sometimes unconsciously see God as being like their fathers. If anyone in your group has difficulty knowing in his or her heart that God's power is just, merciful, kind, and gentle, pray together about that person's feelings toward his or her father. Ask God to reveal Himself as He is, and to enable that person to forgive his or her father and trust God. Encourage the person to consciously forgive his or her father.

On the other hand, some people find God's sovereignty uncomfortable because they want to feel that they run their own lives. Such people need to confess, repent, and acknowledge that God deserves to run the universe.

Finally, other people easily believe in God's love and gentleness, but have trouble believing He is really in control. Such people may feel that God or their earthly fathers have let them down in the past. In particular, deaths and abandonments affect people like this. If anyone in your group feels this way, pray together to see God's sovereign, merciful hand even in the events of your lives that seem unfair, meaningless, and painful. Ask Him to help you stop holding a grudge against Him for apparently letting you down, and ask Him to forgive you for mistrusting either His love or His power.

Summarize. Consider some of these questions: How

143

does 9:14-29 relate to 9:1-13? What potential complaint is Paul answering? What is his main point? What have you learned about God from 9:1-29, and what difference does this make to your lives?

Worship. Praise God for His sovereignty, mercy, patience, power, etc. Ask Him to reveal Himself to you as He really is and lead you to trust both His abilities and His integrity in your lives.

1. *The NIV Study Bible,* page 1719; Cranfield, page 220.
2. *The NIV Study Bible,* page 1719; Cranfield, pages 229-231; Hodge, page 230.

ROMANS 9:30-10:21

Unbelief

In 9:6-29, we have glimpsed God's power and right to choose some people for hardening and others for mercy, some for membership in the Israel-within-Israel and some for exclusion from it. We have seen that the selection is far from capricious; it always serves God's ultimate purpose to display His mercy and saving power among all nations.

However, there is another side to the rejection of most of Israel, in addition to God's sovereignty. In 9:30-10:21, we see Israel's responsibility. Read the passage prayerfully, looking for the train of thought in Paul's reasoning. Try to see how each verse and paragraph fits into the point Paul is explaining.

For Thought and Discussion: Why is it important to keep God's will and man's responsibility in balance in our thinking?

The Jews' attempt (9:30-10:4)

Law of righteousness (9:31). The Old Testament Law is righteous (7:12), and it prescribes the way to be right with God (7:12, 8:4).[1] (Alternatively, "law of righteousness" may mean simply "righteousness" or "principle of righteousness."[2] The interpretation, "righteousness which is of the law," does not fit the grammar of the sentence.[3])

1. God's Law describes how a person can become righteous, and the Jews are correct in pursuing righteousness. However, what is wrong with the

For Further Study:
How did the following
Old Testament people
pursue the Law by
faith rather than
works:
David (Psalms 32, 34,
37, 40, 51);
Isaiah (Isaiah 6:1-8,
8:11-20);
Micah (Micah 6:6-8).

**Optional
Application:** Think
about Paul's attitude
toward unsaved Jews
(Romans 10:1). What
example does this set
for you? How can you
act on 10:1 with
regard to some spe-
cific people, Jewish or
non-Jewish?

**For Thought and
Discussion:** a. Who
is the stone Israel
stumbled over
(9:32-33)?
   b. Why did Israel
stumble over this
stone (10:2-4)?

way Israel pursues the righteousness described
in the Law (9:32)? Explain in your own words.

_____

_____

_____

_____

_____

_____

2. The Jews' pursuit of righteousness is good, but
   their method is not (9:31-32). Likewise, their
   zeal for God is good, but its basis is not
   (10:2-3). What is wrong with the attitude
   behind their zeal to be close to God?

_____

_____

_____

_____

_____

_____

Christ is the end of the law (10:4). The Greek word
telos can mean "termination," "fulfillment," or
"goal." Christ is the termination and fulfillment
of the Law in the sense that: 1) He has fulfilled
its requirements for sacrifice so that we no
longer keep the ritual laws; 2) He has obeyed all
the Law's commands; 3) He has ended its penalties; and 4) He has inaugurated the new covenant (Jeremiah 31:31, 2 Corinthians 3:6), in
which we serve by the Spirit rather than by self-
effort (Romans 7:6).[4]
   However, in Romans 10:1-21, Paul is con-
victing the Jews of utterly misunderstanding
and rejecting that Christ is the *goal* of the Law.
If they had understood God's Law, they would

have recognized that it pointed toward and demanded a Savior to bear man's sin (Galatians 3:24, Colossians 2:17, Hebrews 9:1-14).[5] They would have seen that the laws of sacrifice were meant to lead them to put faith in God's mercy rather than in their ability to earn His favor by works.

Call on the Lord (10:5-13)

Moses said of the commandments, "The man who does these things will live by them" (Romans 10:5, Leviticus 18:5). Israel assumed that God wanted people to strive to keep the commandments in their own strength (Romans 10:3). This was a proud and foolish attempt (Romans 3:20,23; 7:14,21-23).

3. How do Moses' words in 10:5 actually point toward the goal and fulfillment of the Law—Christ (8:3-4)?

_____

_____

_____

_____

_____

But the righteousness that is by faith says . . . (Romans 10:6-8). Again, Paul quotes the Law (Deuteronomy 30:12-14) to show how its real goal is Christ. In Deuteronomy, Moses was countering excuses for disobeying the commandments: no one can say that the commandments are hidden or distant. Paul puts Christ in place of God's Word through the Law to show that what was said of the Law is ultimately true of Christ.

Moses foresaw that the Jews would claim that they failed to obey God's Law out of ignorance, not rebelliousness. Paul foresaw that they would make the same excuse for failing to put faith in Christ.

147

For Thought and Discussion: In a way, the Jews were ignorant of God's way of righteousness (10:2). However, was that ignorance an excuse for lack of faith in Jesus (10:6-8)? Why or why not?

For Thought and Discussion: Do you, or anyone you know, resemble the Jews as 9:31-10:4 describes them? If so, how?

For Thought and Discussion: Why is it so essential to believe that God raised Jesus from the dead (10:9)?

Optional Application: Memorize 10:9-13. With whom could you share what these verses mean and why they are important? Is there someone for whom you could pray, that he or she will soon believe in, confess, and call upon the Lord?

4. What does a Jew, or any person, need to do to be saved (10:9-13)?

_____

_____

_____

_____

_____

Jesus is Lord (10:9). "The earliest Christian confession of faith (compare 1 Corinthians 12:3). . . . In view of the fact that 'Lord' (Greek *kyrios*) is used over 6,000 times in the Septuagint (the Greek translation of the Old Testament) to translate the name of Israel's God (Yahweh), it is clear that Paul, when using this word of Jesus, is ascribing deity to him."[6]

In your heart (10:9). "In Biblical terms the heart is not merely the seat of the emotions and affections, but also of the intellect and will."[7]

5. Why are both *believing* with the heart and *confessing* with the mouth important (10:9-10)?

_____

_____

_____

_____

_____

_____

Why Israel does not call on the Lord
(10:14-21)

Despite 10:6-8, someone might still argue that God did not give the Jews sufficient opportunity to respond to the gospel. Therefore, in 10:14-15 Paul asks four rhetorical questions to show (in reverse logical order) the conditions necessary to call on the Lord and be saved.

6. What are those four conditions?

_____

_____

_____

_____

_____

_____

Optional Application: Who today has had no real chance to hear the good news? Pray persistently that God will send them messengers with the news. Pray with the attitude that you are available if He wants to send you.

How beautiful are the feet (10:15). Isaiah 52:7 describes messengers running to announce to God's people that He is about to deliver them from exile in Babylon. Paul applies the quotation to preachers of the gospel, who proclaim that God has delivered men from sin and death.

According to Paul's quotation of Isaiah 52:7 (Romans 10:15), two of the conditions for calling on Christ have been met in the case of first-century Jews: messengers have been sent, and they have proclaimed the good news.

Lord, who has believed . . . ? (10:16). Isaiah 53:1 is part of Isaiah's song of the Suffering Servant (52:13-53:12), which describes the Servant who would bear the people's sins.

Their voice has gone out (10:18). Psalm 19:4 testifies that the Jews cannot blame their unbelief on a lack of opportunity to hear "the word of Christ" (Romans 10:17).

7. Which condition of salvation was not met in the case of most Israelites (Romans 10:14,16)?

_____

_____

149

_____

_____

I will make you envious (10:19). In Deuteronomy
32:21, Moses foresaw that when Israel became
faithless and idolatrous, God would provoke
them back to faith by means of the Gentiles,
who were not nations in the sense Israel was.

8. Why can't the Jews blame their unbelief on the
fact that they can't understand the word of
Christ (10:19-21)?

_____

_____

_____

_____

_____

_____

_____

Your response

9. What can 9:30-10:21 tell us about . . .

what God does to lead someone to salvation
(10:8,15,21)?

_____

_____

_____

_____

our responsibility for other people's salvation
(10:14-15)?

_____

_____

_____

_____

_____

what a person must do himself to be saved
(10:9-13,17)?

_____

_____

_____

_____

_____

actions and attitudes that keep a person from
salvation (9:32; 10:2-3,6-7,21)?

_____

_____

_____

_____

_____

10. Summarize 9:30-10:21 as clearly as possible.

_____

_____

_____

_____

_____

For Thought and Discussion: According to 9:30-10:21, why does God have a right to choose some people to receive His mercy and some to receive only His justice?

For Thought and Discussion: What did you learn about God and Christ from 9:30-10:21?

151

Optional Application: Pray about your responsibility for others' salvation (question 9). How can you act on this in someone's life this week? Ask God for opportunity and courage.

For Further Study: Add 9:30-10:21 to your outline, or wait until after lesson fifteen.

11. What truth in this passage would you like to apply to your own life?

_____

_____

_____

_____

12. How can you go about applying this truth?

_____

_____

_____

_____

_____

13. List any questions you have about 9:30-10:21.

_____

_____

_____

_____

For the group

Warm-up. Ask everyone to think of someone whom he or she would very much like to see accept the righteousness from God.

Questions. This is a long and difficult lesson because it contains some tough phrases and many Old Testament quotations. Unfortunately, 9:30-10:21 is a logical unit that can't be conveniently broken. Many people have committed themselves to Christ through verses in this passage, but they have never learned how these verses fit into Paul's reasoning about the Jews. This study guide tries to lead you through Paul's logic step by step, and to show how he uses Old Testament quotations without violating their original context. Hopefully, you will be able to trace the points Paul is making and apply them to yourselves in new ways.

Paul claimed that God did send preachers to the Jews of his day, the preachers spoke, and the Jews heard. Therefore, the Jews had every bit as much opportunity as the Gentiles to believe in, confess, and call on Jesus. They even had the Law, which described righteousness by faith and pointed toward Christ. Consequently, the Jews' unbelief was their own fault.

Once your group has grasped what Paul was saying about the Jews, ask yourselves whether the people you long to see saved have had the same opportunities. If not, pray for messengers to bring the gospel, ask God to soften the people's hearts, and make yourselves available to be sent. Critics often complain that God is unfairly condemning people in closed countries who cannot hear the gospel; instead, you might plan as a group to pray for the people of one particular country.

If group members disagree with the interpretations of 9:31 or 10:4 in the study guide, let them voice their views. Many people feel strongly that the Law is utterly abolished in Christ. Encourage group members to come to their own conclusions about this, based on careful examination of the New Testament.

Worship. Praise God for giving people everything they need—the witness of the Law and preachers of the gospel—to lead them to Christ. Praise Him for continuing to provide witnesses. Ask Him to make you messengers of the gospel.

1. *The NIV Study Bible,* page 1720; Cranfield, pages 247-250.
2. Murray, volume 2, page 43; Hodge, pages 329-330.
3. Hodge, page 330; Cranfield, pages 247-248.
4. Bruce, *Romans,* page 203; Hodge, pages 335-336.
5. Hodge, page 335; Cranfield, pages 252-253.
6. *The NIV Study Bible,* page 1721.
7. *The NIV Study Bible,* page 1721.

ROMANS 11:1-36

God's Plan

Chapter 10 may have implied that all Israel has rejected Christ, so God has rejected all Israel. But in chapter 9, Paul explained about the Israel-within-Israel, the Isaacs and Jacobs sovereignly chosen to carry on the inheritance. Now Paul returns to this truth about the remnant to show the present and future purposes of His choices. Read 11:1-36.

Not total (11:1-10)

1. What evidence does Paul cite to show that God has not rejected Israel as a whole, but only the faithless individuals within the nation?

11:1 _____

_____

_____

_____

11:2a (compare 8:29-31) _____

_____

_____

_____

For Thought and Discussion: Is there a difference between saying that a) God has rejected the nation as a whole but saved a remnant, and b) God has rejected unbelieving individuals from the nation but saved the remnant nation as a whole? Why or why not?

For Thought and Discussion: What did the non-elect part of Israel earnestly seek but fail to obtain, and why did they fail (9:30-32, 11:7-10)?

11:2b-5 _____

_____

_____

_____

_____

_____

2. What guarantees the remnant's inheritance of God's blessings (11:5-6)?

_____

_____

_____

_____

_____

Not final (11:11-32)

So as to fall beyond recovery (11:11). "Beyond recovery" is not in the original Greek, and KJV and NASB omit it. However, many commentators agree that this is Paul's meaning.[1]

3. What good resulted from God's sovereign decision to harden most Jews (11:11)?

_____

_____

_____

_____

Fullness (11:12). Possibly, the restoration of the majority of Jews to faith and salvation (11:15,23,26-27,31). This would not mean that no Jews will persist in unbelief, but instead that most will eventually repent.[2]

Alternatively, "fullness" here could mean the completion or coming-to-faith of the elect remnant (full number) of Israel, which may not be a majority of ethnic Jews.

Some people feel that Paul is speaking hypothetically—he longs for the fullness of the Jews, but he isn't sure of it.

4. How will the repentance (and therefore fullness and acceptance) of Israel affect the world (11:12,15)?

_____

_____

_____

_____

_____

For Thought and Discussion: What is the significance of the fact that the Jews did not "stumble so as to fall" (11:11)? (Compare 11:12-16, 23,25-29.)

For Thought and Discussion: a. Inspiring envy is one of Paul's motives for preaching to the Gentiles (11:13-14). How can envy lead a person to faith in Christ?
   b. What are the dangers of appealing to a person's envy?
   c. Is this a method you think you should attempt? Why or why not?

The part of the dough offered as firstfruits (11:16). Each year, the Jews offered to God dough from the first of the harvested grain (firstfruits). This made the whole harvest holy; it belonged to God (Numbers 15:17-21). By analogy, if the patriarchs were set apart as God's people, then the whole nation is also set apart. This does not mean that all will be declared righteous, but it does suggest that their heritage gives them some kind of blessing.[3]

Root . . . branches (11:16). Again, the patriarchs and the rest of Israel. (Ultimately, of course, the patriarchs were rooted in God and Christ. Therefore, some people feel that the root in 11:17-24 is Christ, but the point of the passage is the same.)

5. Paul writes at length in 11:17-32 to overcome an attitude that Gentiles might have. How does he describe this wrong attitude (11:18,20,25)?

**Optional
Application:** a. Do
you ever have the atti-
tude Paul rebukes in
11:18,20,25? Talk to
God about this.
    b. Meditate on
11:18-22. How can
you act on 11:22?

_____

_____

_____

_____

6. Why should Gentiles not have this attitude,
even though God has broken off some Jews from
the tree of His people and grafted Gentiles in
(11:17-24)? Write down as many reasons as you
can find.

_____

_____

_____

_____

_____

_____

_____

_____

Mystery (11:25). Cults in Paul's day used this word
for secrets revealed only to the initiated. However, Paul used it for truths formerly obscure
but now revealed by God for all people to understand. These mysteries are central truths, such
as the Incarnation (1 Timothy 3:16), the death
of Christ (1 Corinthians 2:1-2,7), God's purpose
to sum up all things in Christ and include Jews
and Gentiles in the Church (Ephesians 1:9,
3:3-6), and bodily resurrection (1 Corinthians
15:51).[4]

7. What "mystery" does Paul name in Romans
11:25-27?

_____

_____

_____

_____

_____

_____

For Thought and Discussion: How do you interpret "all Israel" in 11:26? What difference does this make to your life?

For Thought and Discussion: How will "all Israel" be saved (11:26-27)?

All Israel (11:26). Three interpretations of this phrase are:

   1. *"The total number of the elect, both Jews and Gentiles, of every generation."*[5] Against this view, Charles Hodge points out that a) throughout 9:1-11:25 (and especially in 11:25), Paul has been using "Israel" to mean the Jews. (In 9:6-13, Paul wrote of the elect Israel within Israel, but he was not talking about the Gentiles.) Also, b) in 11:28 (and 11:29-32), Paul plainly speaks of God's election of the nation as a whole (although some have rebelled).[6]

   2. *"The total number of elect Jews of every generation."*[7] John Murray objects that a) it is no mystery to say that the elect will be saved, since that is obvious; and b) 11:25-26 brings chapters 9-11 to a climax: Israel's hardening will end and so the nation as a whole (not each individual) will be restored.[8]

   3. *"The great majority of Jews of the final generation."*[9] This would mean that every Jew of that time will be confronted with the truth about Christ and given a choice to believe or reject, and also that most will believe. Stuart Olyott objects that a) the coming of Christ marked the end of God's special interest in the Jews; and b) God does not elect nations, but individuals.[10]

8. In what sense are the Jews "enemies on your [the Gentiles'] account" (11:28)? See 11:11.

_____

_____

Optional Application: How is 11:29 an encouragement to you? How can you respond to this encouragement?

For Thought and Discussion: What does 11:1-32 reveal about God's character?

Optional Application: Think about God's character, as revealed in 11:1-32. How does this passage affect your willingness to trust Him in practical ways?

9. Why is it significant that "as far as election is concerned, they [the Jews] are loved on account of the patriarchs" (11:28)?

10. What is Paul saying about Jews and Gentiles in 11:30-32?

11. How would you summarize 11:1-32?

Doxology (11:33-36)

12. How does Paul describe God in 11:33-36? Note as many observations as you can.

_____

_____

_____

_____

_____

_____

_____

Your response

13. What one truth seems most relevant to you in 11:1-36?

_____

_____

_____

_____

_____

14. How can you take this truth to heart and apply it this week?

_____

_____

_____

_____

_____

_____

_____

For Thought and Discussion: Why is 11:33-36 an appropriate response to 9:1-11:32?

Optional Application: Meditate on 11:33-36 this week. How can you let these truths about God affect your decisions and concerns? Look for at least one concrete way to act on these facts.

For Further Study:
a. Add 11:1-36 or 9:1-11:36 to your outline.
    b. Or, just use the blank pages at the end of the book to outline or summarize 9:1-11:36.

15. List any questions you have about chapter 11.

_____

_____

_____

_____

For the group

Warm-up. Ask each person to think of one way he or she has experienced God's kindness this week, and one way he or she has experienced His sternness.

Questions. Romans 11:26 is hotly debated in some circles. Emphasize that neither anti-Semitism nor a pro-Israeli political policy is necessarily implied by either interpretation. Nor does either interpretation necessarily affirm or deny millenialism. Encourage group members to support their views from Scripture.

Worship. Use 11:33-36 as a basis for your worship. Choose songs that praise God's wisdom.

1. Hodge, page 361; Cranfield, page 274; Luther, page 143; F. L. Godet, *Commentary on the Epistle to the Romans* (Grand Rapids, Michigan: Zondervan Corporation, 1956), page 399. However, see Murray, pages 75-76 for a slightly different view.
2. Hodge, page 362-364; Cranfield, pages 274-275; *The NIV Study Bible*, page 1723.
3. Hodge, pages 366-367; *The NIV Study Bible*, page 1723.
4. *The NIV Study Bible*, page 1724.
5. *The NIV Study Bible*, page 1724.
6. Hodge, page 374. Stuart Olyott notes that in 11:17-24 Paul said that Gentiles were grafted into the tree of Israel. Therefore, it is possible that he is using the name in two different senses in 11:25 and 11:26.
7. *The NIV Study Bible*, page 1724.
8. Murray, page 97.
9. *The NIV Study Bible*, page 1724. This is the view of most commentators: Hodge, page 374; Cranfield, page 282; Warren W. Wiersbe, *Be Right: an expository study of Romans* (Wheaton, Illinois: Victor Books, 1977), page 132; Murray, pages 96-97; Godet, page 411. See Hodge, Cranfield, Godet, or Murray for their reasons.
10. Olyott, pages 104-106.

162

ROMANS 12:1-21

Living Sacrifices

After the song of praise in 11:33-36, what more is there to be said? Nothing but the practical implications of what has gone before. "Therefore" (12:1) ties the rest of the letter to the first eleven chapters; Paul will now explain how we should live "in view of God's mercy" (12:1). Read 12:1-21.

General principle (12:1-2)

1. Explain what you think Paul means by the way he describes our response to God's mercy in 12:1.

offer your bodies _____

_____

_____

_____

_____

as living sacrifices _____

_____

_____

_____

_____

For Further Study:
How has Paul revealed God's mercy in 1:1-11:36? (For example, recall 3:21-26; 4:25; 5:1-2,6-11; 6:22; 7:4-6; 8:1-39; 9:22-25; 10:6-21; 11:1-2,11-16,22-32.)

163

holy and pleasing to God _____

_____

_____

_____

_____

Spiritual (12:1). The normal word for "spiritual" is *pneumatikos* from *pneuma*, "spirit." However, the word in this verse is *logikos* from *logos*, "word" or "reason." It means at once "reason-able" (KJV) and "spiritual"—this worship is the only sensible, spiritual response to God's grace.[1]

Do not conform any longer (12:2). To conform is literally to be molded or stamped according to a pattern. J. B. Phillips renders this phrase (which is both passive and imperative), as: "Don't let the world around you squeeze you into its own mold."[2]

Be transformed (12:2). The Greek verb shows that this is a process, not a single event. Cranfield translates: "continue to let yourselves be trans-formed. . . ."[3] In 2 Corinthians 3:18, this word refers to our inner transformation into Christ's likeness. See also Romans 8:29.[4]

2. According to 12:2, what must happen in order for us to discern and agree with God's will?

_____

_____

_____

_____

3. Name one aspect of "the pattern of this world" that is currently tempting you to conform to it.

_____

_____

_____

_____

_____

_____

4. How can our minds be renewed? (*Optional:* See Romans 8:5,9,12-13; 2 Corinthians 3:18; Ephesians 3:14-21, 4:22-24, 5:1; 2 Timothy 3:16; Luke 11:13; Psalm 1:1-3, 119:11.)

a. What must God do?

_____

_____

_____

_____

b. How must we cooperate?

_____

_____

_____

_____

_____

_____

For Thought and Discussion: Why is "the renewing of your mind" important? (*Optional:* See Romans 1:21,28; 8:5-8; Ephesians 4:17-24; Luke 6:43-45.)

Optional Application: Is there any specific way in which you could apply Romans 12:1-2 with regard to the temptation you named in question 3? If so, how can you put these verses into practice?

Optional Application: Memorize 12:1-2. Make a list of ways you still conform to this world, and ask the Holy Spirit to transform your mind with regard to these. Ask other people to pray for you and help you find relevant Scriptures to meditate on.

Specifics: the Body of Christ (12:3-8)

Having laid down his general principle of life under God's mercy, Paul gives specific exhortations in 12:3-15:13. The first area of our lives in which our thinking needs to be renewed and transformed is how we view our place in the Body of Christ (12:3-8).

For Thought and
Discussion: Paul
emphasizes in several
of his letters that we
are united "in Christ"
(Romans 6:11, 12:5).
What does this
mean? (Consider
Romans 5:15-19,
6:3-11; Ephesians
2:11-22.)

Measure of faith (12:3). Two interpretations are
  possible:
    1. the measured quantity of "power given
  by God to each believer to fulfill various ministries in the church."[5]
    2. the measuring standard of Christian
  faith, according to which all believers are equal
  in God's eyes (Romans 3:22-23, 8:28-30, 9:16; 1
  Corinthians 12:21-26).[6]

5. What facts should keep us from feeling superior
   or inferior to other Christians (12:3-6)?

_____

_____

_____

_____

_____

_____

_____

_____

_____

Gifts (12:6). *Charismata* from *charis*, "grace." God
  gives these gifts by grace through His Spirit to
  enable Christians to meet needs in the Church.

Prophesying (12:6). "A communication of the mind
  of God imparted to a believer by the Holy Spirit.
  It may be a prediction (see Agabus, Acts 11:28;
  21:10-11) . . . an indication of the will of God in
  a given situation (Acts 13:1-2; 1 Corinthians
  14:29-30),"[7] or a word given for "strengthening,
  encouragement and comfort" (1 Corinthians
  14:3).

Serving (12:7). In a general sense, this word covers all service rendered to God or to people in His name. In a specific sense, it means practical service to the needy (Matthew 25:34-40, Acts 6:1-2, Romans 15:25).[8]

Teaching (12:7). "Whereas the prophet of the early Church was immediately inspired, the content of his message being a particular and direct revelation, the teacher based his teaching upon the Old Testament Scriptures, the tradition of Jesus and the catechetical material [teaching material that was eventually put into the New Testament] current in the Christian community."[9]

Encouraging (12:8). As teaching is meant to tell us what is true and what we should do in light of it, so encouragement (or exhortation) is meant to motivate and enable us to do what we have been taught.[10]

Showing mercy (12:8). "Caring for the sick, the poor and the aged."[11]

Optional Application: a. What kinds of needs are the gifts Paul names in 12:6-8 designed to meet? How could you participate in meeting one or more of those needs?

b. Write down one function in your church or the larger Body of Christ that you either are fulfilling now or are able to fulfill. If necessary, ask God to show you at least one function for which He has gifted you. You could also ask your pastor or a close friend.

6. In 12:6-8, Paul lists examples of gifts that may be found among Christians in any given church. The list is not exhaustive, for it is meant to teach principles about how we should use any gift. What principles can you deduce?

_____

_____

_____

_____

_____

_____

7. a. Consider the gifts Paul names in 12:6-8. Which ones are intended for the betterment of the person who has them, and which are

For Thought and Discussion: a. Paul says our love must be "sincere" (NASB: "without hypocrisy"). What does he mean? (For instance, should we not do loving acts unless we feel affectionate toward someone? Why or why not?)

b. Ask God to show you if your love is insincere in any ways.

c. Meditate on some verses from 12:9-21 and look for opportunities to act in sincere love this week. For example, are you sharing with people in need as much as you could (12:13)?

For Thought and Discussion: a. Some Christians emphasize loving people more than hating evil. However, why is hating evil (12:9) equally important?

b. How can one hate evil and not hate the evildoer?

c. Is there any evil in your life that you need to reject in order to cling to good? Ask God to show you if this is so and help you choose the good.

given for the good of the others? (*Optional:* Compare 1 Corinthians 12:7,17-21.)

_____

_____

_____

b. How should this observation affect our attitude toward our own gifts? (*Optional:* See Ephesians 4:11-16.)

_____

_____

_____

_____

_____

8. How should Paul's teaching in 12:3-8 affect your thinking and actions with regard to your function and worth in the Body? Try to name some specific ways in which you want your thinking and will to be renewed.

_____

_____

_____

_____

_____

_____

_____

_____

Specifics: love (12:9-21)

9. In 12:9, Paul speaks for the first time about *our* love. What is the source of our love for fellow Christians and nonChristians (5:5)?

168

_____

_____

_____

_____

For Thought and Discussion: a. What does Paul mean when he tells us to "honor one another above yourselves" (12:10)? (*Optional:* See Philippians 2:2-4.)

b. Think of someone whom you find it hard to honor above yourself (12:10). Why is this hard for you? Look for a way to honor that person this week. Ask the Lord to you a sincere desire to love and honor that person.

10. In what ways is Christian love more than just emotion? See 5:6-8; 12:7-8,10-21; 13:8-10. (*Optional:* See 1 John 3:17-18.)

_____

_____

_____

_____

_____

_____

_____

Spiritual fervor (12:11). Literally, "fervent in spirit" (NASB) or "aglow with the Spirit."[12] Paul is not encouraging bubbling emotion or frantic activity, but joyful action according to the Holy Spirit's guidance.

Hospitality (12:13). This is primarily welcoming strangers and people in need, not entertaining friends. In Paul's day there were no "decent hotels for ordinary people,"[13] so traveling teachers, missionaries, tourists, and business people had to rely on hospitality from friends of friends. Christians were expected to house any Christian that came to the door for a limited period of time. Also, there were no church buildings, so believers offered their homes for worship services. Hospitality to nonChristians may also be implied here. (For further study, see Genesis 18:1-8; 1 Kings 17:7-24; 2 Kings 4:8-14; 1 Timothy 3:2, 5:10; Titus 1:8; Hebrews 13:2; 1 Peter 4:9; 3 John 5-8.)

For Thought and Discussion: a. In 12:12, Paul mentions the renewed mind's approach to affliction. What does he recommend? How can you practice this better?

b. Why should we be joyful in hope when afflicted (12:12)? Remember 5:3-5.

c. If you are currently feeling afflicted, meditate on 12:12 and on your hope (8:18-39). Talk to God about your feelings. Practicing some of the other instructions in 12:9-21 can often relieve the pain of affliction and encourage joyful hope.

Optional Application: Do you find it easy or difficult to associate with people who are poor, mentally deficient, uneducated, or physically handicapped? Meditate on 12:16, and ask God for opportunities to associate with such people so that you can sincerely honor them above yourself.

Do what is right in the eyes of everybody (12:17). Either "Do what all people, even unbelievers, know is right," or "in public, do what you know is right."

Burning coals (12:20). Paul is quoting Proverbs 25:21-22. The statement has several possible meanings, all of which imply repentance. Here are two:

1. In an ancient Egyptian ritual of penance, the guilty person carried a basin of burning coals on his head as a sign of repentance.[14]

2. The coal may depict the pain of shame. This pain of a guilty conscience is intended to drive the enemy to repent and become a friend.[15]

11. Reread 12:9-21 and the optional questions in this lesson. Choose one of Paul's instructions that you particularly need to grow in. Explain what the instruction means.

_____

_____

_____

_____

_____

_____

12. How can you be transformed in this area and act on it during the next week or more?

_____

_____

_____

_____

_____

170

13. List any questions you have about 12:1-21.

_____

_____

_____

_____

_____

For the group

Application. Take a few minutes to share how studying God's sovereignty and mercy in 9:1-11:36, or life in the Church in 12:1-8, has transformed you. How have those passages renewed your minds, wills, attitudes toward circumstances, and behavior?

Warm-up. Ask the group to think of how they are different from nonChristians. Do their attitudes, lifestyles, or behavior set them apart in any ways? This question will prompt thinking about what it means to no longer conform but be transformed.

Questions. The numbered questions leave the specifics of 12:3-21 largely to optional questions. In your discussion, you may want to spend time on one or two of the specifics to see how you can act on them as a group or as individuals. Pray ahead of time about what aspects of chapter 12 your group needs to focus on. Don't let group members just discuss the general principle abstractly without ever commiting themselves to application. But don't lose sight of the fact that the works in 12:9-21 are examples of presenting your bodies as living sacrifices. Give everyone a chance to share how he or she answered questions 11 and 12. This may let you cover most or all of the specifics in 12:9-21.

Verse 20 has long been interpreted as countenancing self-righteous attempts to shame others. This is passive, hypocritical vengefulness, and is wholly inconsistent with the context of the verse. Compare Luke 6:27-42. Ask each group member to recall the person at whom he or she is angry. During your prayer time, ask God to enable you each to fully forgive those people.

For Thought and Discussion: a. Why are the activities in 12:13 crucial for Christians? (*Optional:* See John 13:35, 1 John 3:16-24.)
b. Ask God to give you opportunities to practice hospitality. Talk with Him about the costs involved.

For Thought and Discussion: a. Why is it wrong to repay evil with evil (12:14,17,19-21)?
b. How does doing good to one's enemy overcome evil (12:20-21)?
c. If we pretend forgiveness in order to make another person feel guilty, why haven't we fulfilled 12:19-21?
d. How can we be sure that our kindness to an enemy stems from sincere love?
e. How can you put 12:14,17-21 into practice in a sincerely loving and humble way this week? Ask God to give you an opportunity.

Summarize.

Worship. Thank God for His mercies. Offer yourselves to Him in worship as living sacrifices.

1. Bruce, *Romans,* page 226; Cranfield, page 295.
2. *The New Testament in Modern English,* J. B. Phillips, translator (New York: Macmillan Publishing Company, 1958, 1960, 1972), page 332.
3. Cranfield, page 296.
4. *The NIV Study Bible,* page 1725; Bruce, *Romans,* pages 226-227; Cranfield, page 296.
5. *The NIV Study Bible,* page 1725. However, the amount of our faith is not what is most important to our service (Luke 17:5-6), and faith is always God's gift.
6. Cranfield, pages 300-301.
7. *The NIV Study Bible,* page 1750.
8. Cranfield, page 305.
9. Cranfield, page 305.
10. *The NIV Study Bible,* page 1725; Cranfield, page 305-306.
11. *The NIV Study Bible,* page 1725.
12. Cranfield, page 311.
13. J. N. D. Kelly, *A Commentary on the Epistles of Peter and Jude* (Grand Rapids, Michigan: Baker Book House, 1981 [1969]), page 178.
14. Bruce, *Romans,* page 230; *The NIV Study Bible,* page 981-982.
15. Cranfield, pages 316-317; Wiersbe, page 144; Bruce, *Romans,* page 230; Olyott, page 118; Hodge, page 402.

ROMANS 13:1-14

Debts

The transformed life means serving other Christians in love and humility (12:3-8), and treating strangers and enemies with this same humble love (12:9-21). Chapter 13 continues the theme of the transformed life.

Our debt to the government (13:1-7)

When we read 13:1-7, we should not imagine that Paul was idealistic about governing authorities. The book of Acts shows that he was well acquainted with both the best and the worst of civil government, and also that he practiced what he preached in 13:1-7. Paul had already been imprisoned, given lashings five times by Jewish authorities, and beaten three times by the Romans (Acts 16:16-24, 2 Corinthians 11:24). Therefore, some knowledge about the political situation the early Christians faced can help us see why Paul's counsel made sense then and makes sense now.

The Roman Empire was an authoritarian regime, not a democracy; freedom of speech and assembly were not rights. The government knew religion had political implications, so it recognized certain religions as "legal religions" and the rest as illegal. Judaism was a legal religion, and in 57 AD (when Paul wrote to the Roman believers) Christianity was just another Jewish sect as far as Roman officials could tell. This status was priceless for the Church for many reasons.

173

The Jews were specially exempted from having to offer sacrifice to the emperor as a god, as all subject peoples were expected to do. Instead, the Jews were expected to pray and offer sacrifice for his welfare in their Temple in Jerusalem. This exemption from the emperor cult allowed Jews (and Christians) to maintain their allegiance to one God. However, probably no Christian could hold civil office, for both local and imperial officials had to participate in state religious rites. Furthermore, Christians were considered anti-social and unpatriotic because they declined to join in festivals honoring the gods. Nevertheless, Christians did not mind being barred from office and considered queer by their neighbors as long as they were allowed to worship unmolested. The civil authorities protected the Christian communities as long as they obeyed the law.

However, whenever Paul or another Christian missionary arrived in a town and began to preach the gospel, strife (including quarrels, rioting, and assault) between traditional Jews and Christian converts usually followed (Acts 9:19-31, 14:1-7). Sometimes there was dissension from local pagans whose livelihood was threatened by the missionaries (Acts 16:16-24, 19:23-41). To the Roman officials, it looked as though this sect of Christians was a brood of troublemakers.

Sedition and riot were major threats to the Roman Peace, for in most cities discontented groups were constantly stirring up trouble. Therefore, Rome expected officials to deal with disturbances ruthlessly. Private clubs were always suspected of breeding plots, so they were often banned. There were rumors that in their secret meetings, Christians practiced orgies, incest (the holy kiss between brothers, Romans 16:16), cannibalism (eating someone's flesh and blood, John 6:54, 1 Corinthians 11:23-26), and other vices. On top of everything else, the founder of Christianity was known to have been executed for challenging Caesar's authority (Luke 23:2)! In this climate, Christians meeting in homes and missionaries preaching in rented halls were constantly aware that the government would declare them illegal if they were not model subjects.

Paul knew that there would be times when, like Jesus and Peter, Christians would have to "obey God rather than men" (Acts 5:29). Jesus had been crucified and Paul had been in prison several times for disobeying orders not to preach the gospel. But Paul also knew that when he was arrested, it was crucial that he be able to claim to have obeyed all laws that did not transgress God's Law. As an innocent martyr, he could witness to the faith in a way that would draw converts. As an indiscriminate lawbreaker, he would dishonor God and draw no sympathy when punished.[1]

Read 13:1-7, thinking about how it applies to Christians in both authoritarian states and democracies.

For Thought and Discussion: Some people think that in 13:3-4, Paul is writing only of the ideal function of rulers, not necessarily of what real rulers do. What reasons for and against this interpretation can you suggest?

Submit (13:1). There were three other Greek words that meant flatly "obey," but this word had a different connotation. It was originally a military term that meant to arrange troop divisions in marching order. Thus, to submit was to take one's assigned place because it was assigned, not because of personal inferiority. Submission meant to respect the other person's rank and authority, his place in a chain of command. This included selfless, but not blind and slavish, obedience to the extent of the other person's authority.[2]

1. Why should Christians submit to governing authorities?

   Romans 13:1-2 _____

   _____

   _____

   _____

   13:3-5 _____

   _____

   _____

   _____

175

For Thought and Discussion: Even the oppressive, unjust ruler is "God's servant to do you good" (Romans 13:4). How do cruel rulers like Moses' Pharaoh (Exodus 4:18-14:31, Romans 9:17), Paul's emperor (Nero, who butchered thousands of Christians in 64 AD) and Pontius Pilate (John 19:8-16) serve God's plan and do us good? (See the good Paul describes in Romans 8:28-29. Consider how Pharaoh and Pontius Pilate each served God's plan.)

For Further Study: How did persecution in Jerusalem (Acts 8:1) help to further God's plan (Acts 1:8)?

2. Paul says that if we do what is right, rulers will "commend" (NASB, KJV: "praise") us, even unjust and immoral rulers. How does even an unjust ruler unwittingly commend us if he punishes us for doing good? (*Optional:* See Luke 21:12-15; Acts 16:16-40; Philippians 1:12-14; 1 Peter 2:19-21, 4:12-14.)

_____

_____

_____

_____

_____

_____

3. How do the authorities in your country and locality do you good (Romans 13:4)?

_____

_____

_____

_____

_____

_____

The sword (13:4). The symbol of national defense and internal punishment of criminals. The Roman government was ruthless in maintaining order.

4. Read Acts 4:1-22, 5:17-42.

   a. How did the apostles show submission to the authorities in these passages?

_____

176

_____

_____

_____

_____

_____

_____

_____

b. The apostles disobeyed the clear command of the authorities. Why was this disobedience not a rebellion against the authority God established?

_____

_____

_____

_____

_____

_____

_____

c. What lessons can we draw for our own submission and obedience?

_____

_____

_____

_____

_____

_____

_____

For Thought and Discussion: Paul told Christians to pay taxes (13:6), even though those taxes would support the luxury of pagan officials, oppressive policing of subject peoples, and wars on peoples outside the Empire. Are there any circumstances in which Christians should not pay taxes? If so, why are they justified, in light of 13:1-7? If not, why not, in light of 13:1-7?

For Thought and Discussion: In what ways are a Christian's responsibilities in a democratic state the same as those of a Christian in an authoritarian state? In what ways are his responsibilities different?

For Thought and Discussion: In Romans 13:7, Paul tells us to give everyone what we owe him. To whom do you owe . . .
taxes and revenue?
respect (literally, "fear"; see 1 Peter 2:17)?
honor (Ephesians 6:1-3, 1 Peter 2:17)?
other debts?

For Further Study:
How does Luke
20:20-26 shed light
on Romans 13:7?

**For Thought and
Discussion:** Should
a Christian take part
in revolution or civil
war against an estab-
lished regime? What
about non-violent civil
disobedience? Sup-
port your views from
Scripture.

For Further Study:
Study Paul's submis-
sion to authorities in
Acts 16:16-40,
18:12-18, 21:27-
26:32, 28:17-31.

**For Thought and
Discussion:** What
sorts of actions
communicate love to
you? How can you do
these things for
others?

5. Describe some specific ways in which you can
apply Romans 13:1-7 to your own dealings with
authority.

_____

_____

_____

_____

_____

_____

_____

_____

The debt of love (13:8-10)

Toward laws and public officials, our standard of
conduct is "give everyone what you owe him"
(13:7)—this is *justice*. However, when we deal with
individuals in business and private, we have an even
higher standard; we owe a debt that can never be
fully paid. Read 13:8-14.

6. How does Paul define the relationship between
love and the Old Testament Law of the Ten
Commandments (13:8-10; compare 7:6,22; 8:4)?

_____

_____

_____

_____

_____

Your neighbor (Romans 13:9). The Jews believed
that a neighbor was a fellow Jew, but Jesus

178

taught that a neighbor was anyone in need, or even someone we detest, such as the hated Samaritans (Luke 10:25-37).

As yourself (13:9). As humans, we naturally love ourselves. That is, we may not feel good about ourselves, but we almost invariably put great thought and effort into taking care of ourselves. We are concerned for our own needs. The commandment to love is less about healthy feelings than about this active care and concern.[3]

For Thought and Discussion: What does it mean that "love is the fulfillment of the law" (Romans 13:10; compare Matthew 22:34-40)?

7. Look at the last six of the Ten Commandments (Exodus 20:12-17). For each commandment, write down one positive, loving way it teaches us to treat our neighbors. (In parentheses are New Testament passages that comment on the commandment.)

Exodus 20:12 (Matthew 15:1-9, Ephesians 6:1-4)

_____

_____

_____

_____

_____

_____

Exodus 20:13 (Matthew 5:21-24)
Do not murder: I should respect and enhance my neighbor's life. This includes care for those whose life is threatened by disease, age, handicap, danger or poverty. I must also repent of anger, criticism, resentment, and unforgiveness.

179

Exodus 20:14 (Matthew 5:27-32, Ephesians 5:21-33)

_____

_____

_____

_____

_____

_____

Exodus 20:15 (Luke 6:29-38, 2 Corinthians 9:6-11, Ephesians 4:28)

_____

_____

_____

_____

_____

_____

Exodus 20:16 (Matthew 5:33-37; Luke 21:12-19; Ephesians 4:25,29,31)

_____

_____

_____

_____

_____

_____

_____

_____

Exodus 20:17 (Luke 12:22-34, 16:13; Philippians 4:11-13)

_____

_____

_____

_____

_____

_____

_____

_____

For Further Study: In one sense, we were saved when we were justified by putting faith in Jesus. However, in what sense has our salvation not yet come, but will come soon (13:11)? (*Optional:* See Romans 5:9-10, 8:23; Philippians 3:20-21; Hebrews 9:28; 1 John 3:2-3.)

8. With your answers to question 7 as a guide, describe one specific way you could treat a neighbor or neighbors with love this week.

_____

_____

_____

_____

_____

Understanding the time (13:11-14)

9. Why should we love people beyond the basic debts of justice (13:11-14)?

_____

_____

For Thought and Discussion: Because of our approaching salvation, Paul tells us to do several things. Explain each of the phrases in your own words:

"wake up from your slumber" (13:11). (See 1 Thessalonians 5:1-8.)

"put aside the deeds of darkness" (13:12).

"put on the armor of light" (13:12). (See Ephesians 6:10-18, 1 Thessalonians 5:8.)

"clothe yourselves in the Lord Jesus Christ" (13:14). (See 8:29.)

_____

_____

_____

_____

10. Are any of the deeds of darkness in 13:13 problems for you or people you know? If so, what can you do about them?

_____

_____

_____

_____

_____

11. What is the most significant insight you have had from 13:1-14?

_____

_____

_____

_____

_____

12. What specific action would you like to pursue in response to 13:1-14?

_____

_____

_____

_____

_____

13. List any questions you have about chapter 13.

_____

_____

_____

_____

For the group

Warm-up. Ask, "How do you feel about your local and national government? Are the officials trustworthy, efficient, wise, and so on?" How we feel about particular authorities often affects how easily we accept 13:1-7. It's good to be honest about our feelings, even if we then have to repent of our attitudes.

The government. Have someone recount the political situation Paul and the early Church faced. Then, as you examine each verse in 13:1-7, discuss how God uses even incompetent and tyrannical rulers to do us good and commend our faith. Make sure to consider how 13:1-7 applies to Christians in a democracy, where they are responsible to vote, influence decisions, promote the public good, and even run for office. Discuss the areas in which you resist submitting to governing authorities.

In your prayer time, pray for the grace to submit to authorities, since this is often not easy. If there are specific areas in which you have questions about what you should do, pray about them also. Consider praying for believers in countries where it is very difficult to be a Christian and submit to the state. Pray for your public officials.

You can take a whole meeting for 13:1-7 if you decide to explore some of the optional questions. Encourage group members to jot thoughts in a separate notebook.

Love. To save time, you can discuss just a few of the commandments in question 7. Or, you can make questions 7 and 8 your focus and skim over the others. In a lesson as full as this one, you must either plan extra discussion time or deal with just a few of the issues.

Worship. Thank God for your governing officials. Ask Him to help you appreciate their value and take responsibility to pray for them. Thank God for His commandments and for the nearness of His day of salvation. Pray that the day will come soon, and that He will strengthen you to put off the deeds of darkness and wear the armor of light.

1. Henry Chadwick, *The Early Church* (New York: Penguin Books, 1967), pages 23-29; Ramsay MacMullen, *Paganism in the Roman Empire* (New Haven: Yale University Press, 1981), pages 18-42; Bruce, *New Testament History*, pages 253, 425; Bruce, *Romans,* pages 231-235; Cranfield, pages 317-319.
2. Cranfield, pages 320-321.
3. Cranfield, page 329; *The NIV Study Bible,* page 1726.

ROMANS 14:1-15:13

Weak and Strong

The debt of love applied directly to a situation in the Roman churches, one Paul had faced frequently during the past twenty years. Many Christians were former Jews who believed that God wanted them to obey not just the Ten Commandments but also the Old Testament laws of diet, holy days, and other rituals. They believed that those laws expressed their love for God and gratitude for His grace (Exodus 20:1-17, Mark 12:28-31). Unlike certain groups whom Paul opposed, these Jewish Christians did not try to earn righteousness by obeying the laws, nor did they insist that Gentile Christians obey them. These Jewish Christians were simply unclear about "the status of the Old Testament regulations under the new covenant inaugurated by . . . Christ,"[1] so they kept the regulations for conscience's sake.

However, some Gentile Christians regarded this keeping of customs as a denial of the New Covenant, and they questioned their Jewish brethren's faith in Christ. At common meals, they may have made a point of serving foods forbidden by the Law of Moses, and they pointedly ignored Jewish holy days. For their part, the Jewish Christians were shocked at behavior they were brought up to consider immoral, and they doubted their Gentile brothers' full conversion from paganism and dedication to holiness. The Jewish believers were also greatly confused as to what was truly right and wrong, but the scorn of Gentile believers made it difficult for the Jewish ones to sort out answers. Issues of custom

185

and ritual threatened to dwarf more serious matters of evangelism, worship, and mutual upbuilding.

In this situation, Paul set about writing to people who knew him by reputation as a zealous opponent of legalism (Galatians 1:1-6:18, Philippians 3:1-4:1). The Romans may have expected him to scold the Jewish Christians for clinging to their customs. However, read 14:1-15:13.

1. What is Paul's overall message in 14:1-15:13 to . . .

   "strong" Christians (those who don't feel obliged to keep dietary laws and holy days)?

   _____

   _____

   _____

   _____

   _____

   _____

   "weak" Christians (those who do feel obliged)?

   _____

   _____

   _____

   _____

   _____

   _____

2. What reasons does Paul give for not judging other people on "disputable matters" (14:1)?

   14:3 _____

   _____

   _____

   14:4 _____

   _____

14:9-12 _____
_____
_____
_____
_____
_____
_____

For Thought and Discussion: What are some things we should do before we decide that Scripture is not explicit on an issue, and that therefore it is a disputable matter?

For Thought and Discussion: When Scripture is not explicit on an issue, how should a person decide what is right and wrong? (See 13:8-10, 14:15-19.)

Vegetables (14:2). Most butcher shops in Paul's day were attached to pagan temples. The animals were ritually sacrificed to the gods, some of the meat was burned, and the rest was sold to the public. Jewish communities had their own butchers to assure meat that had never been sacrificed to idols, but they may have refused to sell to Jewish Christians with scruples about buying pagan meat. Therefore, some Jewish Christians may have become vegetarians rather than eat meat sacrificed to idols.[2] (Compare 1 Corinthians 8:1-11:1.)

Also, there were religious groups, both Jewish and pagan, who considered all meat unclean for food. Reasons for this taboo varied from sect to sect, but a person who converted from such a group may have had difficulty doing something he had long been taught was wrong.

3. If you aren't sure whether something is right or wrong, should you do it? Why or why not (14:14,23)?

_____
_____
_____
_____
_____

4. If you are sure that something is acceptable (neither required nor forbidden), what considerations might make it wrong to do in certain circumstances?

14:13-15,20-21 _____

_____

_____

_____

_____

_____

14:16 _____

_____

14:19 _____

_____

_____

For Thought and Discussion: How could doing what another person mistakenly thinks is wrong make him vulnerable to committing sin (14:21)?

For Thought and Discussion: Why is it especially important for Jewish and Gentile Christians to bear lovingly with each others' scruples (15:8-12)?

For Thought and Discussion: In 15:4,13, Paul speaks about hope, not love or faith. How is hope necessary for the accepting, self-denying behavior Paul urges in 14:1-15:13?

For Thought and Discussion: In what ways is 15:4 relevant to our lives, other than as a support to 15:3?

Kingdom of God (14:17). The reign of God that is both a present reality in our lives and, in its fullness, a future hope.

Bear (15:1). "Not merely to tolerate or put up with but to uphold lovingly."[3]

Failings (15:1). "Infirmities" in KJV; "weaknesses" in NASB. "Not sins, since in the matters under discussion there is no clear guidance in Scripture."[4]

5. Why should Christians bow to other people's scruples? (What truths about Christ and His Kingdom should motivate us?)

14:15 _____

_____

188

14:17-18 _____

_____

_____

_____

_____

_____

15:1-3 _____

_____

_____

_____

_____

15:6 _____

_____

_____

6. Why should a Christian lovingly accept others who do something he considers foolish, when Scripture does not specifically address the activity (15:7)?

_____

_____

_____

_____

7. Paul prays for unity (likemindedness) among Christians (15:5). Does unity mean that believers must come to the same opinions or convictions about everything (14:1,5,22)? If so, why? If not, what does unity mean?

_____

For Thought and Discussion:

a. According to 14:1-15:13, should a missionary in India avoid meat because many Hindus think eating meat is immoral? Why or why not?

b. Should a Christian woman in a Moslem country cover herself as Moslem women do? Why or why not?

c. Is it right to drink alcohol among those who abstain for moral or personal reasons (14:21)? Why or why not?

d. How should Christians decide what activities are proper on Saturday and Sunday, in light of the variety of views regarding the Sabbath? Is 14:1-15:13 relevant, or is Scripture clear on this subject?

e. What are some other "disputable matters" (14:1) in our day? How can we decide?

Optional Application: a. What matters are topics of dispute within your church, or between you and others?

b. Investigate what the whole of Scripture says about these topics. Ask someone to show you how to use a concordance, topical Bible, and other aids.

c. Ask God to give you love, acceptance, and a willingness to be spiritually united although in disagreement with the others.

d. Meditate on verses from 14:1-15:13 that seem relevant.

e. Look for practical ways to demonstrate your acceptance of the others.

Optional Application: How does 14:23 apply to the lifestyle issues you are currently facing?

Optional Application: Pray the prayers of 15:5,13 diligently for yourself and others.

8. As we struggle to decide what is right and wrong, and to accept people we disagree with, what encouragement do we have?

15:4 _____

_____

_____

_____

_____

15:5 _____

_____

_____

_____

_____

15:13 _____

_____

_____

_____

_____

9. Reread 14:1-15:13, and jot down the insights that you would like to apply and the areas of your life to which they are relevant.

_____

_____

_____

_____

_____

_____

_____

_____

_____

For Further Study:
Use some of the
blank space at the
end of this book to
outline 12:1-15:13.

10. What meditation, prayer, and/or practical
action can you pursue to apply one of these
insights this week?

_____

_____

_____

_____

_____

_____

_____

11. Write down your questions regarding
14:1-15:13.

_____

_____

_____

_____

For the group

Warm-up. Say, "Think of one area of disagreement
between you and other Christians with whom you
work, live, or worship."

Questions. People who know Paul's letter to the
Galatians often ask why he doesn't simply explain to

the "weak" believers why they don't need to keep dietary rules and holy days. After you study 14:1-15:13, see if you can answer this question. The reason is subtle and will illuminate Paul's views on love and unity among believers.

Make a list of as many issues as you can think of that are debated in the Church. Divide this list under two headings: 1) disputable matters on which Scripture is not explicit, and 2) issues on which Scripture gives clear guidance but some Christians (in your view) are not submitting to Scripture. How should you deal with the people you disagree with on each matter? On which issues are you "strong" Christians, and on which are you "weak"? (Or, do these labels not apply, and why not?) Would the people you disagree with on any of these issues consider you "weak" and themselves "strong"? Is it important to know who is "strong" and who is "weak" when you disagree?

Consider some of the following topics:

food	medical technology
dress	music (leisure)
make-up	music (in church)
dating	the Sabbath (Sunday)
sex	women's roles
alcohol	tithing
film	capital punishment
television	spiritual gifts
abortion	political involvement
disarmament	baptism and communion

Worship. Thank God for cultural diversity among Christians. Praise Him for being each believer's Master, so that we don't need to judge each other. Thank Him for endurance, encouragement, and unity (15:5). Thank Christ for becoming "a servant of the Jews on behalf of God's truth" (15:8). Glorify God for His mercy.

1. *The NIV Study Bible,* page 1727.
2. Cranfield, page 336.
3. *The NIV Study Bible,* page 1728.
4. *The NIV Study Bible,* page 1728.

ROMANS 15:14-16:27

Personal Words

Back in chapter 1, Paul introduced himself as an apostle of the gospel, dedicated to leading Gentiles to the obedience of faith. Now Paul has thoroughly explained the gospel he preaches, and he is ready to return to the business that prompted this letter. These personal comments give us a window into Paul's character and motives, and into the workings of the early Church. Read 15:14-16:27.

For Thought and Discussion: How does 15:8-12 help to introduce 15:14-33?

Paul's plans (15:14-33)

1. How does Paul see his own mission (15:15-16)?

_____

_____

_____

_____

_____

2. To what does Paul credit his immense success in evangelism (15:18-19)?

_____

_____

_____

193

Optional Application: a. What grace has God given you (15:15-16)? What do you glory in (15:17-19)?

b. How can you seek to adopt and put into practice one of the attitudes you named in question 4?

Optional Application: What is your greatest ambition? How does it compare with Paul's (15:20)?

3. What attitudes toward himself and his mission does Paul express in 15:16-22?

_____

_____

_____

_____

_____

_____

_____

Signs and miracles (15:19). See Acts 14:8-10; 16:16-18,25-26; 20:9-12; 28:8-9; 2 Corinthians 12:12.

Illyricum (15:19). A Roman province north of Macedonia. Modern Yugoslavia. (See the map on page 9.)

4. Why has Paul never been able to visit Rome (15:19-22)?

_____

_____

_____

_____

_____

5. Why is he now planning to go there (15:23-24)?

_____

_____

_____

_____

6. Before visiting Rome, Paul has to deliver his churches' gift to the believers in Jerusalem (15:25-29). How does Paul want the Roman Christians to help him (15:24,30-32)?

_____

_____

_____

_____

_____

_____

7. Is there anything in 15:14-33 that you would like to apply in your own life? If so, what is it, and what do you plan to do about it?

_____

_____

_____

_____

_____

_____

For Thought and Discussion: a. What have the Jews done for the Gentiles (11:11; 15:8-9,27)?
b. How should the Gentiles therefore treat the Jews (15:26-27)?
c. In what ways is Paul's attitude toward Jewish and Gentile Christians (15:8-12,16,26-27) a model for our behavior toward Jews or other groups?

Optional Application: How can you do for some missionary what Paul wanted the Roman Christians to do for him (15:24,30-32)? Why is this kind of help important?

Pray that I may be rescued from the unbelievers in Judea (15:31). Paul wanted to present the Gentile Christians' gift in person, so that he could explain that it was not just alms but an expression of love from Gentile to Jewish Christians. However, he knew that danger awaited him from the nonChristian Jews in Jerusalem (Acts 20:22-23).[1]

Greetings (16:1-23)

Our sister Phoebe (16:1). A fellow believer. She probably bore the letter from Corinth to Rome, since Paul is commending her to the Romans.

195

Servant (16:1). The Greek word is *diakonos*, so RSV, NIV margin, and NASB margin give the alternate translation, "deaconess." The word originally meant one who waits on (serves at) tables, but Christians came to use it for one who serves the sick, needy, and widows (Acts 6:1-6, Romans 12:7). In light of 1 Timothy 2:8-3:13, many people feel that Phoebe could not have held an office of deaconess that was equivalent to the male office of deacon. However, 1 Timothy does not restrict women from the function of minister to the needy.[2]

Cenchrea (16:1). Corinth and Cenchrea were twin port cities, six miles apart on either side of the isthmus of Corinth. Ships were often hauled overland from one port to the other to avoid sailing around Greece. (See the map on page 9.)

A great help (16:2). This Greek term sometimes meant specifically hospitality and financial support, but it could also have the wider sense of service in general.

Priscilla and Aquila (16:3). A (probably) Jewish woman and her Jewish husband who had worked with Paul in Corinth (Acts 18:1-2). They had left Rome in 49 AD when Emperor Claudius expelled all Jews, but now Claudius was dead, his edict had lapsed, and Priscilla and Aquila were back in Rome.

Junias (16:7). This is probably a feminine name,[3] although we cannot be certain.[4]

Outstanding among the apostles (16:7). Two interpretations are possible:

1. Andronicus and Junias are "apostles" in the wider sense of the word—a distinct group of missionaries of the gospel recognized by the churches (Acts 14:4,14; 1 Corinthians 12:28; Ephesians 4:11; 1 Thessalonians 2:6).

2. Andronicus and Junias are outstanding "in the opinion of" the Twelve Apostles whom Jesus named.[5]

The two were Jewish ("my relatives") and had become Christians before Paul ("they were in Christ before I was"), so it is likely that they converted in Jerusalem not long after the Resurrection, knew the Twelve, and may even have seen the risen Jesus. Whether we take interpretation (1) or (2), they must have been exceptional workers for Christ to have won this praise from Paul.

Tryphena and Tryphosa . . . Persis (16:12). All women. The first two are probably twin sisters.

For Thought and Discussion: Nine of the twenty-seven people Paul names in 16:1-15 are women. What does this fact imply about Paul's relationships with women?

8. Paul praises several people in 16:1-15 for things they have done. What deeds and qualities does he commend?

_____

_____

_____

_____

_____

_____

9. Think about how Phoebe, Priscilla, Aquila, and the rest are models for you to follow. What one quality of these people would you like to adopt, and how can you do this?

_____

_____

_____

_____

_____

_____

10. In 14:1-15:13, Paul wrote about divisions of opinion that Christians should allow. However, what kinds of divisions should churches not allow (16:17)?

For Thought and Discussion: What feelings does Paul express toward his fellow Christians in 16:1-16? How is this an example for you?

Optional Application: Is 16:17-20 relevant to your church in any way? If so, how? What can you do to help mend this situation?

11. What does Paul say about the sort of person who causes these bad divisions (16:17-18)?

_____

_____

_____

_____

_____

12. How should Christians deal with this sort of person (16:17)? (*Optional:* See Matthew 18:15-17 and 1 Corinthians 5:11.)

_____

_____

_____

_____

_____

Tertius (16:22). Paul's secretary. In the ancient world, it was common to have someone else write from one's dictation.

Gaius (16:23). Probably Paul's host in Corinth (Acts 18:7, 1 Corinthians 1:14); his full name would have been Gaius Titius Justus.

Erastus (16:23). Corinth's "director of public works" (NASB: "treasurer"; KJV: "chamberlain") was a very important man, an aristocrat. Despite numerous scholarly efforts to deduce the proportion of highborn versus lowborn people in the early Church, all we can say for certain is that there were plenty of slaves and freedmen (16:14-15), tradespeople and artisans (16:3), wealthy businesspeople (Gaius, 16:23), and perhaps a few local aristocrats like Erastus. This distribution (a large number of slaves, freedmen, and tradespeople, along with a smaller number of rich people and even fewer aristocrats) roughly mirrored the proportions of each class in the nonChristian world.[6]

For Further Study:
Finish your outline of Romans.

Doxology (16:25-27)

13. Paul closes with ringing praise to God, appropriate to the majesty of his letter. What does he say about . . .

    God? _____

    _____

    _____

    _____

    _____

    the gospel (the message he has explained and means to preach in Spain)?

    _____

    _____

    _____

    _____

    _____

14. List any questions you have about 15:14-16:27.

    _____

    _____

_____

_____

_____

For the group

Warm-up. Ask the group, "What is your greatest ambition?" When you get to 15:20, compare your ambitions to Paul's.

Questions. Look for ways to help the group identify with Paul in his ambitions, the Gentile Christians in their generosity, Phoebe in her service, Priscilla and Aquila in their willingness to take risks, and so on. As you look at each person and group, discuss practical ways in which you can serve, contribute, evangelize, etc. Encourage each member to choose one area for practical action. Is there anything you can do together, as did the saints in Macedonia and Achaia (15:26), or as Paul wanted the saints in Rome to do (15:24,30-32)?

Worship. Thank God for apostles like Paul and believers like those in Rome. Use 16:25-27 as a springboard to praise.

1. *The NIV Study Bible*, page 1730.
2. Bruce, *Romans*, page 270; Hodge, page 447; Cranfield, page 374; Wiersbe, page 172; *The NIV Study Bible*, page 1730.
3. *The NIV Study Bible*, page 1730; Cranfield, page 377.
4. Bruce, *Romans*, page 271; Hodge, page 449.
5. Cranfield, page 377; *The NIV Study Bible*, page 1730; Hodge, page 449.
6. Wayne A. Meeks, *The First Urban Christians* (New Haven, Connecticut: Yale University Press, 1981).

REVIEW

Looking Back

Now that you've studied the letter to the Romans, do you understand it well enough to explain the gospel? If your memory of the book isn't crystal clear, a review can help. It can also remind you where to look up the details when you need them and which passages you might want to restudy later.

Begin by rereading the whole letter, if possible. It should be familiar by now, so you should be able to skim rapidly, looking for the threads that tie the book together. Pray for a fresh perspective on what God is saying.

Also, review the overview lesson, any outlines you made, and the summaries you wrote for each passage. All this will help to jog and organize your memory. If it seems like too much work, do as much as you can with the time and skills God provides.

Study Skill—Returning to the Purpose
Many teachers of Bible study stress the importance of returning to the author's purpose after studying a book. Our view of the overall purpose often changes after a close look at the details.

J. I. Packer calls this the "spiral" approach to Bible study: from overview to details and back to overview, spiraling in on the book's message. The better we understand the overall message and intent of the book, says Packer, the better context we have for interpreting and applying the details.

---

1. In question 5 of the overview (page 18), you said tentatively what you thought was the theme of Romans. After closer study, how would you now summarize Paul's main reasons for writing this letter? (*Optional:* See 1:1,14-17; 15:15-16,23-24.)

_____

_____

_____

_____

_____

_____

Study Skill—Answering Others' Questions

Many Christians understand the gospel well enough to put faith in Christ, but not well enough to help others believe. The book of Romans answers many questions that unbelievers and new Christians ask. Try to answer questions 2 through 8 in simple language that an unbeliever could understand, avoiding or explaining words that nonChristians might misconstrue. (For example, people use terms like "righteous" and "self-righteous" differently from Paul.) Imagine that you are answering a friend who does not know the Bible.

2. What is righteousness?

_____

_____

_____

_____

_____

3. Why aren't we born righteous (1:18-32, 5:12-19)?

_____

202

_____

_____

_____

_____

_____

4. How can we become righteous (3:21-26, 5:15-21)?

_____

_____

_____

_____

_____

_____

5. Why can't we become righteous by doing good (1:28, 2:1-6, 3:9-20, 5:12-14, 7:7-25)?

_____

_____

_____

_____

_____

_____

_____

6. Why is a Christian not free to sin if he wants, even though his sins are forgiven (6:1-23)?

_____

_____

_____

_____

For Thought and Discussion: Do all people deserve to be saved and go to heaven? Why or why not?

Optional Application: Explain the gospel to someone by drawing on Romans.

For Thought and Discussion: Define these words: sin, grace, faith, justification, atonement, sanctification, flesh, spirit. Use terms an ordinary person could grasp.

203

For Thought and Discussion: a. What were some of the functions of the Old Testament laws before Christ came (3:2,20,21; 5:20; 7:7-13; 10:4-11; 13:9-10)? (Compare Galatians 3:21-25.)

b. What place does the Old Testament Law of the Ten Commandments have in a Christian's life (13:9-10)?

c. What place do the Old Testament laws of sacrifice and religious custom have in a Christian's life (3:21, 10:4)? (Compare Hebrews 9:9, 10:1.)

For Thought and Discussion: What did Jesus do for us, and how did He do it (3:25; 4:25; 5:1,10,15-19)? (Compare Hebrews 8:1-10:18.)

For Thought and Discussion: a. What place do the Jews have in God's plan (9:1-11:32)?

b. How is 9:1-11:32 crucial to the overall message of Romans?

_____

_____

_____

7. How is it possible to become holy and obey God (6:11-14, 7:1-8:39)?

_____

_____

_____

_____

_____

_____

_____

8. Briefly, what guidelines does Paul give for Christian living in relationship to . . .

other Christians (12:1-21, 13:8-15:13)?

_____

_____

_____

_____

_____

_____

the state, government officials, and civil laws (13:1-7)?

_____

_____

_____

_____

_____

_____

nonChristians, including enemies (12:1-2,9-21;
13:8-14)?

_____

_____

_____

_____

_____

_____

9. What were the most important truths you
   learned from Romans about . . .

   God the Father? _____

   _____

   _____

   _____

   _____

   Jesus Christ? _____

   _____

   _____

   _____

   _____

   _____

For Further Study: If you like, use the blank pages at the end of this study guide to outline the entire book of Romans in as much depth as you want.

the Holy Spirit? _____

_____

_____

_____

_____

_____

10. Review the questions you listed at the end of lessons one through nineteen. Do any remain unanswered? If so, some of the sources on pages 209-213 may help. Or, you might study some particular passage with cross-references on your own, or ask a pastor or teacher.

11. Have you noticed any areas (thoughts, attitudes, opinions, behavior) in which you have changed as a result of studying Romans? If so, how have you changed?

_____

_____

_____

_____

_____

_____

_____

12. Look back over the study at questions in which you expressed a desire to make some specific application. Are you satisfied with your follow-through? Pray about any of those areas, or any new areas, that you think you should continue to pursue. Write any plans here.

_____

_____

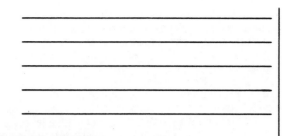

For the group

Warm-up. Tell the group, "Think of one person to whom you would like to explain the gospel. Choose someone you know at least slightly, but this person does not need to be someone you can imagine evangelizing tomorrow. Keep this person in mind when the group discusses questions 2-8."

Review. If the group has trouble with the idea of the book's purpose, try restating the question: What is the book about? How do 1:18-3:30, 3:21-5:21, 6:1-8:39, 9:1-11:36, 12:1-15:13, and 15:14-16:27 fit into the letter's theme and purpose? Modern readers often have the most trouble seeing how 9:1-11:36 is crucial to the overall message, so be sure everyone understands why this section is relevant.

Many people find it very hard at first to answer questions about the gospel without using language that is unfamiliar outside Christian circles. Help each other find ways of explaining concepts like salvation, sin, righteousness, justification, atonement, flesh, spirit, spiritual, grace, love, election, calling, legalism, faith, etc. in ordinary English. (The group can choose just a few terms to explore.)

Your goal in questions 2-8 and the "For Thought and Discussion" questions is to be able to answer the very basic questions that unbelievers and new believers often ask. You could have one group member pretend to be a Christian explaining a concept, while the rest pretend to be nonChristians trying to understand. Take turns being the explainer. The "nonChristians" should try to ask questions that encourage further explanation of unclear points. Don't be distressed if you can't state the ultimate answers. If this practice for evangelism seems helpful, consider taking a second meeting to finish.

Give everyone a chance to raise unanswered questions, and take a few minutes to point toward answers. The leader should avoid answering whenever possible. Instead, he or she should either let someone else answer or suggest books or passages of Scripture that can give answers. It is a good rule for the leader never to do for the group what it can do for itself. This rule encourages the whole group to mature and work together. (Of course, a leader should intervene if the group is misunderstanding a passage.)

Questions 12 and 13 allow you to evaluate how you have grown from studying and applying Romans. This is not a time to feel guilty or self-satisfied, but a time to be encouraged, re-motivated, and enabled to keep going. If you don't see many results yet, ask yourselves whether you should do or pray or think about application differently, but don't assume that you are doing something wrong. Transformation and the renewing of the mind does not happen overnight. You may just need to persevere in your present approach to application and trust God for results.

Evaluation. You might want to take a few minutes or a whole meeting to evaluate how your group functioned during your study of Romans. Some questions to consider are:

What did you learn about small group study?
How well did the study help you grasp Romans?
What were the most important truths you discovered together about the Lord?
What did you like best about your meetings?
What did you like least? What would you change?
How well did you meet the goals you set at your first meeting?
What are members' current needs? What will you do next?

Worship. Praise God for specific things you learned about Him during your study of Romans. Thank Him for His plan of salvation, the righteousness from God, the gospel of Jesus. Thank Him for the opportunity to study His Word together. Thank Him for specific ways He has changed each of you during your study.

208

STUDY AIDS

For further information on the material covered in this study, consider the following sources. If your local bookstore does not have them, ask the bookstore to order them from the publisher, or find them in a seminary library. Many university and public libraries will also carry these books.

Commentaries on Romans

Cranfield, C. E. B. *Romans: A Shorter Commentary* (Eerdmans, 1985).
    Cranfield's two-volume commentary on Romans (International Critical Commentary) is considered one of the best scholarly commentaries on Romans ever written. This *Shorter Commentary* in one paperback volume is ideal for the layman because it omits the Greek text and most footnotes and references to scholarly works. On debatable passages, Cranfield usually lists the main interpretations and evaluates each. Insightful, orthodox, and clearly written.

Hodge, Charles. *Commentary of the Epistle to the Romans* (Eerdmans, 1947 [1864]).
    This old standard is still extremely valuable for researching particular passages. Hodge quotes the Greek text and often even Latin sources, but the English reader can still follow his reasoning.

Murray, John. *The Epistle to the Romans*, two volumes in one (New International Commentary on the New Testament, Eerdmans, 1968 [1959, 1965]).
    Somewhat more difficult writing style than Cranfield, but still a fine work. Greek text and references are in footnotes.

Olyott, Stuart. *The Gospel as It Really Is: Paul's Epistle to the Romans Simply Explained* (Evangelical Press, 1979).

An easily read exposition of what Olyott thinks the letter means. By ignoring the "trees" of particular phrases and alternate interpretations, Olyott helps the reader see the "forest" of Romans. As with all commentaries, the reader is likely to disagree with Olyott at points, but the book is still worthwhile for those who want a simple overview, explanation, and applications to the present.

Stott, John. *Men Made New: An exposition of Romans 5-8* (Inter-Varsity Press, 1966).
A clear, careful explanation and contemporary application of these key chapters for ordinary readers.

Wiersbe, Warren. *Be right: an expository study of Romans* (Victor Books, 1977).
Another simple explanation that avoids close phrase analysis and alternate interpretations. Practical for the average reader.

Historical Sources

Bruce, F. F. *New Testament History* (Doubleday, 1979).
A history of Herodian kings, Roman governors, philosophical schools, Jewish sects, Jesus, the early Jerusalem church, Paul, and early Gentile Christianity. Well documented with footnotes for the serious student, but the notes do not intrude.

Bruce, F. F. *Paul, Apostle of the Heart Set Free* (Eerdmans, 1977).
Possibly the best book around on the historical background and chronology of Paul's life. Bruce explains Paul's personality and thought from an evangelical perspective, although some readers will disagree with his interpretation at points.

Harrison, E. F. *Introduction to the New Testament* (Eerdmans, 1971).
History from Alexander the Great—who made Greek culture dominant in the biblical world—through philosophies, pagan and Jewish religion, Jesus' ministry and teaching (the weakest section), and the spread of Christianity. Very good maps and photographs of the land, art, and architecture of New Testament times.

Concordances, Dictionaries, and Handbooks

A *concordance* lists words of the Bible alphabetically along with each verse in which the word appears. It lets you do your own word studies. An *exhaustive* concordance lists every word used in a given translation, while an *abridged* or *complete* concordance omits either some words, some occurrences of the word, or both.

The two best exhaustive concordances are *Strong's Exhaustive Concord-*

ance and *Young's Analytical Concordance to the Bible*. Both are available based on the King James Version of the Bible and the New American Standard Bible. *Strong's* has an index by which you can find out which Greek or Hebrew word is used in a given English verse. *Young's* breaks up each English word it translates. However, neither concordance requires knowledge of the original language.

Among other good, less expensive concordances, *Cruden's Complete Concordance* is keyed to the King James and Revised Versions, and *The NIV Complete Concordance* is keyed to the New International Version. These include all references to every word included, but they omit "minor" words. They also lack indexes to the original languages.

A **Bible dictionary** or **Bible encyclopedia** alphabetically lists articles about people, places, doctrines, important words, customs, and geography of the Bible.

The New Bible Dictionary, edited by J. D. Douglas, F. F. Bruce, J. I. Packer, N. Hillyer, D. Guthrie, A. R. Millard, and D. J. Wiseman (Tyndale, 1982) is more comprehensive than most dictionaries. Its 1300 pages include quantities of information along with excellent maps, charts, diagrams, and an index for cross-referencing.

Unger's Bible Dictionary by Merrill F. Unger (Moody, 1979) is equally good and is available in an inexpensive paperback edition.

The Zondervan Pictorial Encyclopedia edited by Merrill C. Tenney (Zondervan, 1975, 1976) is excellent and exhaustive, and is being revised and updated in the 1980's. However, its five 1000-page volumes are a financial investment, so all but very serious students may prefer to use it at a church, public, college, or seminary library.

Unlike a Bible dictionary in the above sense, *Vine's Expository Dictionary of New Testament Words* by W. E. Vine (various publishers) alphabetically lists major words used in the King James Version and defines each New Testament Greek word that KJV translates with that English word. Vine's lists verse references where that Greek word appears, so that you can do your own cross-references and word studies without knowing any Greek.

Vine's is a good basic book for beginners, but it is much less complete than other Greek helps for English speakers. More serious students might prefer *The New International Dictionary of New Testament Theology*, edited by Colin Brown (Zondervan) or *The Theological Dictionary of the New Testament* by Gerhard Kittel and Gerhard Friedrich, abridged in one volume by Geoffrey W. Bromiley (Eerdmans).

A **Bible atlas** can be a great aid to understanding what is going on in a book of the Bible and how geography affected events. Here are a few good choices:

The MacMillan Atlas by Yohanan Aharoni and Michael Avi-Yonah (MacMillan, 1968, 1977) contains 264 maps, 89 photos, and 12 graphics. The many maps of individual events portray battles, movements of people, and changing boundaries in detail.

The New Bible Atlas by J. J. Bimson and J. P. Kane (Tyndale, 1985) has

73 maps, 34 photos, and 34 graphics. Its evangelical perspective, concise and helpful text, and excellent research make it a very good choice, but its greatest strength is its outstanding graphics, such as cross-sections of the Dead Sea.

The Bible Mapbook by Simon Jenkins (Lion, 1984) is much shorter and less expensive than most other atlases, so it offers a good first taste of the usefulness of maps. It contains 91 simple maps, very little text, and 20 graphics. Some of the graphics are computer-generated and intriguing.

The Moody Atlas of Bible Lands by Barry J. Beitzel (Moody, 1984) is scholarly, very evangelical, and full of theological text, indexes, and references. This admirable reference work will be too deep and costly for some, but Beitzel shows vividly how God prepared the land of Israel perfectly for the acts of salvation He was going to accomplish in it.

A *handbook* of Bible customs can also be useful. Some good ones are *Today's Handbook of Bible Times and Customs* by William L. Coleman (Bethany, 1984) and the less detailed *Daily Life in Bible Times* (Nelson, 1982).

For Small Group Leaders

The Small Group Leader's Handbook by Steve Barker et al. (InterVarsity, 1982).
    Written by an InterVarsity small group with college students primarily in mind. It includes information on small group dynamics and how to lead in light of them, and many ideas for worship, building community, and outreach. It has a good chapter on doing inductive Bible study

Getting Together: A Guide for Good Groups by Em Griffin (InterVarsity, 1982).
    Applies to all kinds of groups, not just Bible studies. From his own experience, Griffin draws deep insights into why people join groups; how people relate to each other; and principles of leadership, decision making, and discussions. It is fun to read, but its 229 pages will take more time than the above book.

You Can Start a Bible Study Group by Gladys Hunt (Harold Shaw, 1984).
    Builds on Hunt's thirty years of experience leading groups. This book is wonderfully focused on God's enabling. It is both clear and applicable for Bible study groups of all kinds.

How to Build a Small Groups Ministry by Neal F. McBride (NavPress, 1994).
    This hands-on workbook for pastors and lay leaders includes everything you need to know to develop a plan that fits your unique church. Through basic principles, case studies, and worksheets, McBride leads you through twelve logical steps for organizing and administering a small groups ministry.

How to Lead Small Groups by Neal F. McBride (NavPress, 1990).
    Covers leadership skills for all kinds of small groups—Bible study, fellowship, task, and support groups. Filled with step-by-step guidance

and practical exercises to help you grasp the critical aspects of small group leadership and dynamics.

DJ Plus, a special section in *Discipleship Journal* (NavPress, bimonthly).
Unique. Three pages of this feature are packed with practical ideas for small groups. Writers discuss what they are currently doing as small group members and leaders. To subscribe, write to Subscription Services, Post Office Box 54470, Boulder, Colorado 80323-4470.

Bible Study Methods

Braga, James. *How to Study the Bible* (Multnomah, 1982).
Clear chapters on a variety of approaches to Bible study: synthetic, geographical, cultural, historical, doctrinal, practical, and so on. Designed to help the ordinary person without seminary training to use these approaches.

Fee, Gordon, and Douglas Stuart. *How to Read the Bible For All Its Worth* (Zondervan, 1982).
After explaining in general what interpretation (exegesis) and application (hermneneutics) are, Fee and Stuart offer chapters on interpreting and applying the different kinds of writing in the Bible: Epistles, Gospels, Old Testament Law, Old Testament narrative, the Prophets, Psalms, Wisdom, and Revelation. Fee and Stuart also suggest good commentaries on each biblical book. They write as evangelical scholars who personally recognize Scripture as God's Word for their daily lives.

Jensen, Irving L. *Independent Bible Study* (Moody, 1963), and *Enjoy Your Bible* (Moody, 1962).
The former is a comprehensive introduction to the inductive Bible study method, especially the use of synthetic charts. The latter is a simpler introduction to the subject.

Wald, Oletta. *The Joy of Discovery in Bible Study* (Augsburg, 1975).
Wald focuses on issues such as how to observe all that is in a text, how to ask questions of a text, how to use grammar and passage structure to see the writer's point, and so on. Very helpful on these subjects.

Titles in the LIFECHANGE series: